JACOB'S SHADOW

JACOB'S SHADOW

Christian Perspectives on Masculinity

by Herbert Anderson

Bridge Resources
Louisville, Kentucky

Unless otherwise noted, Scripture quotations are from the New Revised Standard Version of the Bible, copyright 1989 by the Division of Christian Education of the National Council of the Churches of Christ in the U.S.A. Used by permission.

Grateful acknowledgment is made to the following for permission to reproduce copyrighted material. From *Plainsong* by Kent Haruf, copyright © 1999 by Kent Haruf. Used by permission of Alfred A. Knopf, a division of Random House, Inc. From *Letters and Papers from Prison*, Revised, Enlarged Edition by Dietrich Bonhoeffer. Reprinted with the permission of Simon & Schuster, Inc. Copyright © 1953, 1967, 1971 by SCM Press, Ltd. *Cat's in the Cradle*, by Harry Chapin and Sandy Chapin, © 1974 Story Songs, Ltd. All rights reserved. Used by permission of Warner Bros. Publications U.S. Inc., Miami, FL. 33014.

Every effort has been made to trace copyrights on the materials included in this book. If any copyrighted material has nevertheless been included without permission and due acknowledgement, proper credit will be inserted in future printings after notice has been received.

Edited by Cassandra D. Williams

Book interior and cover design by Jeanne Williams

Cover art and interior illustrations by Doug Purnell

First edition

Published by Bridge Resources
Louisville, Kentucky

Web site address: http://www.bridgeresources.org

PRINTED IN THE UNITED STATES OF AMERICA

02 03 04 05 06 07 08 09 10 11 — 10 9 8 7 6 5 4 3 2 1

Library of Congress Cataloging-in-Publication Data

Anderson, Herbert, date.
  Jacob's shadow : Christian perspectives on masculinity / by Herbert Anderson. — 1st ed.
    p. cm.
Includes bibliographical references.
  ISBN 1-57895-101-1 (pbk.)
  1. Men—Religious life. 2. Masculinity—Religious aspects—Christianity. I. Title.
  BV4528.2.A53 2002
  248.8'42—dc21

                                             2002009218

*This book is dedicated to four generations
of men in my family:*

*To my grandfather, Johan Anderson,
for teaching me by his example
how to endure sadness,*

*To my father, Ernest Anderson, who
combined selflessness and
compassion in fulfilling his pastoral
responsibilities,*

*To my son, Joel Anderson, who demonstrates
by his life as a father, husband, and
teacher that the head and the heart
can be integrated,*

*To my son-in-law, Gilbert Febos, who has
shown me the nurturing heart of
a father, and*

*To my grandson, Jonah Anderson, whose
curiosity at age three about
dinosaurs and Fordson tractors
is a wonder to behold.*

TABLE OF CONTENTS

ACKNOWLEDGMENTS

More people have contributed to this book than I can remember or name. I am grateful for all the conversations, formal and informal, with men and women that have deepened and expanded my thinking about the issues with which men struggle. Some people who have read written material and offered confirmation and critique must be thanked by name: Joel Anderson, Ed Crouch, Gilbert Febos, Bob Fitzgerald, Freda Gardner, James Halfaker, Gerard Jancoski, Richard Jensen, Dennis Johnson, Victoria Kill, Todd MacIntyre, Rod MacKenzie, Don Mayer, James Nold, Eldon Olson, Mark Saline, Gary F. Skinner, Paul Tillquist, Tom von Fischer, Christine Wenderoth, Mark Wiberg, and Robert Wilson. Australian artist and pastoral theologian Doug Purnell has been a faithful long-distance friend and conversation partner. James Eblen is a remarkable man and friend who has also been a source of amazing insights on the Jacob story. I am very grateful that my wife, Phyllis Anderson, continues to handle with kindness the *angst* that accompanies my writing. Much of what I have learned about being a man has been formed by our life together. My deepest appreciation is for Curt Miller, former Associate for Men's Ministry of the Presbyterian Church (U.S.A.), for the invitation to write this book and for his extraordinary patience in the process of completing the project.

INTRODUCTION

Some time ago, in 1997 to be precise, I was invited by the Office of Men's Ministries of the Presbyterian Church (U.S.A.) to write a book about men. I readily accepted the invitation as an opportunity to reflect on being a man in the midst of a gender revolution. I did not anticipate what I would experience after taking on that writing task. In December of that year, my wife, Phyllis, accepted a position in Seattle, Washington, far from my employment in Chicago. For the second time in our marriage, her job determined where we lived. It was not a difficult choice to make. For the previous thirteen years, my wife had provided the primary income. Because other values are present, decisions in marriage about whose vocation is primary are not economically determined. In this situation, to insist on keeping my job even though it paid poorly, was not only unjust but unwise. So we bought a home in Seattle and I continued to teach in Chicago for two more years. It was a long commute. Even though the move was clearly the prudent and just thing to do, it was not easy.

I learned again through this process that justice is not so much something we achieve as something we discover. The discovery of justice depends on seeing one another's gifts clearly, articulating individual hopes and dreams, and in my situation, being willing to make common cause with one's spouse for a deeper vision of a just relationship. For those who follow Christ, justice is gift rather than something earned. Justice is therefore linked to gratitude. Discovering justice by sharing power is only one of the issues that the transition from Chicago to Seattle stirred in me. I did not, however, write this book during the summer of 1998 as I had planned. I painted the house instead. It gave me an excuse to avoid reflecting on those changes in my life and the lives of men today that I hope to address in this book. Generally, men are more inclined to act than reflect. One purpose for this book is to invite thinking about being a man from the perspective of faith in God.

I also became a grandfather for the first time in 1998. Grandchildren are a gift of new life and an occasion for joy. It is not just that we are free to love grandchildren without the responsibility of raising them: their presence points to a future that transcends the present. This sense of the future is also why grandchildren are a burden. I wish for my grandchildren a world in which each of them is free to choose which gifts to actualize and which dreams to pursue. I hope that by the time my grandchildren are adults, we will have navigated our way through the present uncertain waters of gender identity to new role clarity and enduring mutual respect between women and men. The presence of grandchildren in my life compels me to work for a peaceable world in which the similarities between women and men build trust and the differences are occasions for celebration and creativity rather than fear and occasional violence.

In May 1999, I was diagnosed with prostate cancer. I heard the results of the biopsy by phone while standing in the kitchen of our home in Seattle, a paintbrush in my hand. It was the day before my sixty-third birthday. I was stunned by the diagnosis because there had been no history of cancer of any kind on either side of my family. I had uncles who lived well into their nineties. Mercifully, I did not throw the paintbrush. The next day, however, a friend of mine and I cut down three trees on our little city lot and carted four pickup truckloads of leaves, branches, and assorted debris. Prostate cancer (or the fear of it) touches deeply the masculine center of power for most men. I will say more about this in a later chapter. This will not be, I promise you, a book about prostate cancer. However, insofar as that reality is now a permanent part of my experience, it shapes how I think about being a man. Going through treatment for prostate cancer became another excuse to put off writing this book.

I retired from teaching at Catholic Theological Union in Chicago in the spring of 2000 after thirty-one years of teaching pastoral theology in schools of ministry. I shipped seventy-five boxes of books and took a train to my new home in Seattle. My great fear of retirement was that I would fall into a dark hole and be forgotten forever. I managed to schedule enough activities for the remainder of 2000 to postpone the fulfillment of that fear or the full realization of retirement. Those activities also functioned as another excuse to avoid writing this book. Once it became clear that I was not likely to fall into the dreaded "retirement hole," new energy for writing about men emerged.

BEYOND OLD MYTHS THAT WHISPER AND SHOUT

During my lifetime, the women's movement has challenged me to think in new ways about being a man. During that same time, I have learned new ways to connect the liberating power of the Christian faith with my life as a man. When my wife and I were married in 1964, I gave her a hymnal and had engraved on the cover "Mrs. Herbert Anderson." It was a loving act consistent with the traditional expectations of being men and women that I had learned in a traditional Christian family. Male headship in my family's household did not require biblical documentation; it was simply assumed. When I decided to go to graduate school and move my wife and son across the country with *no* financial security, it was what we did. My dream was our destiny. That was what my father had done all his life. My wife was very sad and a little angry about giving up the role of minister's wife that she had come to relish as her ministry. Today, she has an identity of her own that does not derive from being my wife. When I think about the beginnings of my marriage and ministry, they seem very far away. And yet from far away the old myths of male dominance continue to whisper and shout.

It is hard not to do what our fathers did. Even when I consciously intend to act differently than I remember my father acting, I still sometimes do things just about the way he did. Our fathers are the most powerful models we know for what it is to be a man. Even by their absence they have taught us what it means to be a man. For many today, being a man still means to keep our distance, ignore pain, overcome fear, swallow our tears, keep our options open, and maintain an upper hand whenever we can. These are the old myths that continue to whisper and shout. Because those messages are so powerful, they are not easy to ignore. We long for a new vision of what it means to be a man. We still have work to do to fashion a world in which both women and men will be free to celebrate their full humanity with mutual respect. For that reason I consider it a privilege to write a book that invites men to take such a vital but sometimes difficult journey in the certain hope that with God human transformation is always possible.

My struggle with writing this book is a parable for the resistance many men experience to explore new ways of being. If men think about changing, it is easy to become fearful that the loss will be greater than the gain. That fear of loss may make men reluctant to acknowledge even the changes they know need to be made. Many voices have been critical of men in the last decades, insisting they change in one way or another. Sometimes men have been criticized for behavior that is the logical extension of actions for which men have also been praised. For example, the inability of men to express feelings is in part the consequence of being expected to maintain a steady, even stoic, presence in the midst of chaos. My initial resistance to expressing myself through a book is in part a result of being brave and peaceable during prostate cancer treatment. One aim of this book is to explore new ways of being a modern man of faith without repeating the critical judgments of men for what they are not. I hope you will find this to be an empathic approach to the changes men might consider making that will enhance the fullness of our being human.

FINDING A NEW WAY

The publication of this book is itself an indication that we are less certain than we used to be about what it means to be a man. The assumptions that underlie traditional masculinity have been questioned from many perspectives. Some of the challenges to traditional masculinity have come from women as they have found ways to express the pain of living for centuries under male dominance. In turn, women have challenged men to discover deeper dimensions of their humanity that do not depend on dominance for either power or authenticity. Other questions about traditional male/female roles are a consequence of modern advances in technology that have, for example, made many forms of labor accessible to both women and men. The impetus for change also comes from men themselves who feel trapped in stereotypes of masculinity that no longer fit. Men want to be free to develop personal characteristics according to individual gifts or preferences rather than gender prescription. Finally, hearing the Christian gospel proclaimed is a regular invitation to see masculinity through a different lens.

One response to these challenges to men's ways of being has been to reassert male dominance and insist on maintaining traditional male roles whenever possible. It is sadly true that known violence by men toward women has increased rather than decreased in our society in recent decades. Some of that violence is about conflicts between people rather than between genders. However, much of male violence or abuse against women can be attributed to frustration with feeling powerless or humiliated in a system that men once dominated and some men still expect to dominate. Entitlement dies slowly. Even if the evidence is indisputable that many male stereotypes are hurtful to women and children and finally to ourselves, some men persist in holding on to a position they insist is a right.

Another response is to take the feminist critique seriously. When I do, I often end up feeling guilty but still not yet motivated to change. Some years ago I had an unsettling conversation with a woman that ended with her saying I was a "son of Pharaoh" and "likely to remain so." I did not want to hear that I would be a tyrant all my life. What I wanted from her was an absolution and then a suggestion about how to change. I got neither. I realized some time later that it was not her responsibility to tell me how I should act. This book is an effort to suggest new alternatives to the old destructive stereotypes. Finding a new way is the work men must do for themselves. I believe that the local congregation is an ideal place to do such work. It is where men are challenged by Christian virtues of respect, honesty, and vulnerability, surrounded by supportive partnerships, and sustained by the liberating assurance of God's grace.

Yet another response has been to look for new ways in old stories. Many writers have attempted to rediscover the ancient myths as a way of articulating genuine masculinity.[1] While the recovery of ancient myths may help men gain new clarity about the origins of modern understandings of masculinity or become aware of the deeper longings for the secrets of power or spiritual worth, those images still carry ancient presumptions of patriarchy and other expressions of male dominance. Attempting to redeem male images from the past is appealing in this time of change, but it will not ground us in a Christian understanding either of humanity or manhood. The development of a masculine spirituality away from old male images toward a new mode of being needs to be informed by a biblical vision of being human.

In his book *Fire in the Belly*, Sam Keen has suggested that "the image of Jesus on the Cross is central to the Christian notion of manhood because it dramatizes the issue of will, a recurring theme in any discussion of manhood. . . . The lesson of Gethsemane is that a man is most virile not when he insists upon his autonomous will but when he harmonizes his will with the will of God."[2] The boldness and virility of Jesus sometimes seems far away from men today who are inclined to understand autonomy as self-will rather than obedience to the will of God. The aim of Christian faithfulness for men and women alike is to fashion lives in harmony with the will of God. Another aim of this book is to foster patterns and practices of being a man that embody that expanded vision of being human.

WRESTLING WITH A STRANGER: JACOB'S STRORY AND OUR STORIES

The biblical story of Jacob is the framework for this book. Jacob is not a simple character. He is weak and wise, strong and naive, prayerful and stubborn. Jacob is a man for our time precisely because we can see ourselves in his ambiguity, we are comforted by his flawed humanity, and yet we are inspired by his persistent faithfulness. Modern men of faith still live in Jacob's shadow. I hope you will find the same resonance with the biblical character of Jacob. What I have learned from the Jacob story is that the journey to faithfulness in God is a bumpy road full of struggle and unexpected change. Jacob needed to give up well-established patterns of acting and relating to be faithful to God. The unavoidable shattering of some of those male symbols of privilege and power will continue beyond my lifetime. What we begin will take generations to complete. Even so, it is urgent that we begin, even though the way to the end is not clear. Just being on the way will make a difference for our lives and for those who follow.

Each chapter of this book begins with a segment from Jacob's life that foreshadows the struggles of men today. We discover in Jacob's story themes that point men today in new directions. These new qualities or practices that men need to foster or develop more fully are examined critically in relation to similar characteristics that have dominated our understanding of being a man. For example, learning to grieve more effectively will depend on modifying the importance of self-control in men. The equation of strength with power will need to make room for greater awareness of human vulnerability and different kinds of strength and power. In the ancient myths, men presumed power without vulnerability. What we know more clearly today is that men are in fact most powerful when they are most vulnerable and most vulnerable at the height of their power. The practice of being a man in our time is therefore both exciting and difficult.

The ten themes that are treated in the following chapters have evolved over years of reading and reflecting on the stories of men. These ten themes do not, however, include every issue that men face. Readers will have other themes to add from their own experience. If this book were written for women, there would be a different list of qualities and practices previously ascribed primarily to men that women need to learn. Because the qualities and practices that have defined being a man or being a woman are socially constructed over time, they can be changed. Gender roles are not genetically predetermined. That is a hopeful word. However, though gender role change is possible, it is not easy. For that reason, I use two strong words—dangerous and struggle—to describe the process of deepening and expanding our humanity as men.

Because there is no necessary logic to the sequence of the chapters, you may follow your own order in reading the chapters. If you begin with the theme that touches you most personally, you will be more likely to continue reading. If one chapter does not connect with your experience or takes you into deeper waters than you wish to go, try another. Most of all, I hope this book will provoke discussion and the desire to gather with a group of men to reflect together on deepening our humanity as Christians. A local congregation is the best context I know to engage in that reflection with other men who are also willing to risk telling their stories. At the end of this book, there are some questions that might help initiate those conversations. The important thing is to begin. "A journey of a thousand miles starts from beneath one's feet."

Introduction

The image of Jacob wrestling with "a stranger in the night" whom he later understands to be God captures the struggle of men to become more deeply human and faithful to God. Jacob wrestling is a particular moment in his life but it is also thread throughout his life and this book. The sketches by Doug Purnell on the cover and at the beginning of each chapter invite us to be aware of the people with whom we struggle, the spiritual or moral anguish that keeps us awake, or the private battles we wage with unspoken demons and with God as we seek to claim full manhood as men of faith. Because my conversations with Doug Purnell about being men have significantly influenced my thinking, these drawings are more than illustration. They are among the many perspectives that have shaped this book. I am grateful to Doug for what he has inspired in me about imagination and about being a man.

In an essay entitled "The Story of Jacob's Wrestling with an Angel," Jewish writer Edward Hirsch describes wrestling with God: "To be like Jacob one must wrestle all night with a stranger and know him to be an angel. One must struggle with an unknown, unnamed fate and then go forth in the morning, wounded, thankful, and refreshed."[3] Writing is like that, Edward Hirsch observes. It is a way of engaging the mysteries. Writing this book has been a similar experience of "engaging the mysteries" of my life in new and liberating ways. I hope that reading this book will be such an experience for you—an encounter with known and unknown fates, wrestling in the night with unknown angels so that in the morning you can go forth wounded, transformed, thankful, and refreshed for a life of faithfulness.

The LORD of hosts is with us;
the God of Jacob is our refuge.

Psalm 46:11

PROLOGUE

Jacob's story begins before his birth. He came from an influential family with a remarkable legacy: Abraham was his grandfather and Isaac his father. He was a child of God's promise to make a great people. High expectations undoubtedly surrounded the birth of Esau and Jacob because their parents had waited so long for children. Even before the twins were born, Rebekah reported a struggle in her womb. When she asked for an interpretation of this womb activity, Rebekah was told that two nations would be formed from these yet unborn sons. This story and the divine prophecy about it most likely would have been told the twins as they grew up. But even if the story was never told, it would have shaped how Rebekah (and Isaac, if he knew) responded to Esau and Jacob. The promise of conflict preceded their birth. It was in the actual story of their birth, however, that the twins got their names and, in a sense, their destiny. "The first came out red, all his body like a hairy mantle; so they named him Esau. Afterward his brother came out, with his hand gripping Esau's heel; so he was named Jacob" (Gen. 25:25–26). The prologue to his birth and how his birth occurred is a significant part of Jacob's story.

Every human life is a story in the making. Even when we do not intend to, we are fashioning our lives into stories to help us organize and make sense of our experiences. In telling our stories, we construct the unique character of our lives. Most people are eager to tell their stories in order to be understood and build community with others. Men, however, are sometimes reluctant to tell stories about their lives. Some of those stories are about failure or war and are too painful to tell. Other stories are not told because they are awkward or embarrassing and reveal too much vulnerability. When fathers cannot tell the stories of their origins, sons and daughters are left to guess about the significant influences or events in their development. When men are silent, we must create narratives of their lives from the outside by interpreting actions and activities. Men will often justify their silence by insisting that actions speak louder than words. I hope this book will encourage men to fashion their stories from the inside out.

STORIES BEFORE OR ABOUT OUR BIRTH

We begin our exploration into our origins with family stories that precede our birth. Each particular narrative will have a prologue that introduces themes and characters and predictable patterns of responding that set the stage for what follows. Like Jacob, whose grandfather was the patriarch Abraham, our family prologue might include a famous person, or it might contain a succession of shopkeepers in the county seat. Like Jacob, the pregnancy preceding our birth might have been difficult or remarkable enough to be told as a prologue to our story. Or, like Jacob, the birth itself or how we were named may be part of our narrative as well. Each of us is born into a narrative that precedes us. It is part of our story.

> Stories are the currency of our humanness. They are like stones with which you can build the mansion of your own life. By reading about the lives of other men, we can broaden our definition of what masculinity means, love with more assurance, deepen our sense of humanity, and be part of the collective project to build a world worth living in.
>
> Steve Biddulph,
> *Stories of Manhood*

My origins are rural, Swedish, and Lutheran. My father's ancestors in Sweden immigrated from Finland in the seventeenth century at the invitation of King Gustavus Adolphus to create more tillable soil in western Sweden by deforesting the land. Generations later, those ancestors immigrated to the United States and eventually settled in North Dakota, again leaving behind familiar territory to follow a dream. My father left his home farm in North Dakota at age twenty-five to begin high school and prepare to be a pastor. My grandfather never understood why my father had to leave the soil behind. Without intending to imitate the past, my life has followed the pattern of the prologue. I am a Lutheran pastoral theologian, but most of my teaching career has been in Presbyterian and Roman Catholic schools of ministry. I currently continue my pastoral work in the Episcopal Church. Like generations before me, I have left familiar territory to fulfill my calling.

We cannot rewrite the prologue or history before our birth. Nor can we change our beginnings or alter the expectations that preceded us. How we respond to these expectations is, however, our responsibility. In a poem called "The Jacob Cycle," Presbyterian pastor David Steele described the influence of Jacob's origins with this verse.

> Each child inherits, so it seems
> A bundle of parental dreams.
> And Jacob, master of deception,
> Will find that he is no exception.[1]

The divine interpretation of the womb struggle between Esau and Jacob before their birth would have been part of the "bundle of parental dreams" each boy inherited. Before the twins were born, Rebekah had been told that "one shall be stronger than the other [and] the elder shall serve the younger" (Gen. 25:23). How and why Esau and Jacob were named was another inheritance each boy received that undoubtedly shaped their lives. These names were quite specific to the circumstances of the birth.

The name given a child may also carry family expectations. I was named for the young brother of my mother who died tragically in a farm accident at age twelve. As long as I can remember, I was also told that Herbert, the boy for whom I was named, was a very sensitive child. My second name, Ernest, was my father's first name and carries the weight of being intense about life. Given those names and the expectations surrounding them, it is not surprising that I have been an overly responsible, serious-minded person from early in life and remain so to this day. Discovering the significance of our name or names is one way to reclaim the stories of our origin or the expectations for our future. If we can identify parental dreams and expectations in our prologue, we are more likely to change living patterns that confine us.

PARENTAL DREAMS THAT PRECEDE US

The stories before or about our birth should provide a platform from which we choose our way in the world. Sometimes, however, the stories of our origins limit our freedom and determine what path we take, what occupation we choose, or how successful we become. For most of us, the legacy we receive is a mixture of freedom and destiny. A friend of mine reflected on the day of his birth in this way: "My world—all nine adults—were gathered to tell me who I was to be, to predict, to adore, to demand, to celebrate, to love, and mostly to define." As his life unfolded, each of those nine adults continued to love and adore him as the only child among them and seek to define who he was to become. My friend's struggle throughout his life to find his own vocation and his own freedom amidst all the dreams defining his life is a common story among men. The stories of our birth or about how we were named carry those expectations and have power to shape our own journey. Learning the stories of our origins later may be painful, messy, or awkward but understanding those stories empowers us to refashion a life in personal, authentic ways.

The needs and claims of parents also influence the legacy that precedes our birth. From birth, Esau and Jacob each had a special relationship with one parent that reinforced the parental expectations and the distinctive gifts each brought into the world. Esau joined his father in farming and hunting while Jacob was mother's helper in the kitchen. Therefore "Isaac loved Esau, because he was fond of game; but Rebekah loved Jacob" (Gen. 25:28). Isaac probably had high expectations that his son Esau would become successful in a foreign land in a way he, Isaac, had not. These early alliances between parents and children are established when children are very young, channel a child's interests, and actively direct the formation of identity. As we see clearly in Jacob's story, the devotion of one parent may significantly shape the identity and destiny of a child.

According to the biblical story, it was Jacob's mother, Rebekah, who initiated the trickery that cheated Esau out of his birthright. Jacob was a willing instrument in his mother's ambition to achieve the highest blessing for *her* favorite son. It is no different today. One son may be expected to fulfill a parent's dream, inherit the family farm or take over the family business, hold certain political views, or keep secrets as an act of loyalty to one parent or both parents. Kahlil Gibran's admonition to parents in *The Prophet* is quite specific: "You may house their bodies but not their souls, for their souls dwell in the house of tomorrow, which you [parents] cannot visit, not even in your dreams."[2] It is a great temptation for parents to seek to create a future for our children according to our own "bundle of parental dreams" and not their gifts or dreams. Sometimes parents give divine justification to such interference. Like many mothers since, Rebekah may have believed that orchestrating Jacob's future by deceiving Isaac was part of God's plan.

For most of my early life, I was my mother's helper and confidant. It was my assignment as a young boy, as I now understand it, to be her support and keep her from depression. Even when I was married and a father, after enough education and therapy to know better, I made choices that put my own family at risk because of the strength of that emotional claim. My mother interpreted my father to me and then drafted me into an alliance against him. Loyalty to my mother also prevented me from having a close relationship with my father until after my mother died. Becoming a man can be complicated partly because we may have to modify the emotional claims or reject the expectations of parents that seek to define or control us in order to be free to discover our own gifts, form our own identity, and determine our own destiny. The "bundle of parental dreams" we inherit may help us move toward personal maturity and clarity about being a man, or those dreams may inhibit our growth and restrict our freedom to be all we could be. In either instance, each man's narrative begins before birth.

STORIES OF OUR FATHERS

Stories of our birth or parental expectations for our future are not the only sources of influence before our birth. The personal story of our beginnings is added to a stream of stories of fathers, grandfathers, uncles, and others that provides images of what it means to be a man. This is another way our destiny is shaped even before we begin the journey. Over the years, some of these stories may have been embellished to enhance the heroics or rearranged to remove smudges or serious sins. As a result, we are sometimes inspired by extraordinary legends or by pictures of masculinity without vulnerability. Or stories are not told because all the women agree that the men in the family are irresponsible, prone to alcoholism, unable to hold a steady job, silent and distant, or susceptible to violence. Some sons grow up with a hole in the soul not knowing about fathers who died young or who left their mothers when the boys were children. Unfortunately, too many boys inherit secrets fiercely kept in silence instead of stories of their fathers that inspire and inform.

We do not know, for example, what stories Isaac told his sons about Abraham, the legendary man of faith for the people of Israel, who planned to sacrifice Isaac to please God. In his novel about Jacob called *Son of Laughter*, Frederick Buechner includes a vivid account of Abraham's near sacrifice of his only son, Isaac, told from Isaac's perspective. As Isaac tells his son Jacob about his grandfather Abraham, there is no bitterness or hatred in the story, only profound sadness and these words:

> [Isaac] said, "When my mother heard what Abraham had nearly done to her son, she was dead within the year. What killed her? You tell me.

And when you tell me what killed her, then you can tell me what killed me. . . . I was not always the way you see me now." It was then that Laughter [Isaac] fell down by the smoldering dung with his face buried in his arms and lay there as if he were dead.[3]

The narrative that precedes Jacob's birth includes the story of Abraham's obedience to God, even to the sacrifice of his only son, but it also includes banishing the slave woman's son and stories of Isaac's broken life, Abraham's child of promise, who never quite measured up to his father's expectations. Almost every family legacy is like that: a mixture of failure and success, of strong and weak men, of destinies fulfilled and promises unmet. In that sense, we still live in Jacob's shadow.

I did not know my mother's father because he died when she was young. Uncles on my mother's side were mostly quiet farmers who read the Almanac, belonged to the Farmer's Union, dressed up for church, and let hard work talk for them. Although my father's father lived until he was almost ninety, I did not know him well. He was a sad man who had been a widower for fifty-seven years. My own father was a Lutheran pastor who worked long hours. In his ministry, he was patient, compassionate, and overly conscientious. As a result, he was often busy or too preoccupied to be present in the family. I wish I had known him better. While my father lived, he was reluctant to speak of his achievements and even more reticent to speak about his inner world. When he died, I was the recipient of his diaries. I expected, at last, to know my father. What I learned from the diaries was more about his public life. My father was still hidden from view. Like many fathers, he taught me about being a man through silence and hiddenness. Along the way, I equated hiddenness with masculinity. The story is both the same and very different for boys who do not know who their fathers are or for men whose fathers were both physically and emotionally absent. Whether the absence is physical, emotional, or both, it is a difficult lesson to unlearn.

CULTURAL STORIES OF MANHOOD

The stories from our fathers and grandfathers about being a man are part of larger cultural narratives that have presumed male superiority, promoted manly courage, and supported the dominance of men for centuries and centuries. Until recently, it was assumed women needed to become more like men to be fully human. Until recently, it was believed that masculinity was the result of nature more than of nurture. Until recently, images of what it means to be a man were dominated by John

Wayne, Muhammad Ali, Rambo, or George Jefferson in *The Jeffersons*, and Archie Bunker in *All in the Family*. Real men, we were led to believe, pump iron, work hard, talk tough, ignore feelings, like football, never cry, and don't eat quiche. We understood that masculinity meant keeping distance, overcoming fear, ignoring pain, swallowing tears, celebrating action over thought, and maintaining the upper hand whenever we could. We cannot change that history but we need not be trapped by it.

There are plenty of cultural stories that perpetuate this dark side of the history of men. There are stories of the exploitation of the earth, the humiliation of women, and violence for the sake of dominance. Even if we choose to understand being a man differently than ancient stereotypes or popular culture, those images are prologue to our own story and part of our larger cultural narrative. It is easy to imagine how men became dominant. When human work and social progress depended on physical strength, men had the edge. Men also had more freedom to hunt and move about because their procreative responsibility was not as confining as women's task of bearing and raising children. Because these patterns of dominance have continued for such a long time, some men still assume they are the aggressors and intended to dominate relationships because it is their nature.

> There is much talk these days of the new, liberated man being a "feminized" man; men are told to aspire to greater openness of feelings and tenderness, so that they will become "more like women"—somehow reciprocating women's efforts to be stronger, "more like men." But I think that living up to the new specifications is at least as deadly as living up to traditional specifications.
>
> James Dittes,
> *The Male Predicament: On Being a Man Today*

In *Iron John*, a popular and influential book about men, the poet Robert Bly insists that the images of men from popular culture are worn out.[4] Our male mythologies no longer work, he argues, because they ignore depth of feeling and teach obedience to the wrong powers. Bly invites modern men to trust the ancient myths that tell us how men are and ought to be because these myths are free of modern psychological prejudices. The ancient myths invite modern men to rediscover the "wild man" within the male psyche. Regrettably, Robert Bly's understanding of forming a masculine self is unnecessarily negative toward women. Furthermore, it requires taking the influence of ancient myths more seriously than most modern men do. Old mythologies of kings and magicians seem out of place in a world of faxes and e-mail. Even so, these mythic stories are part of the prologue to the story of modern men. Acknowledging the ancient narratives that precede our birth is necessary in order to be free from the claims of those ancient myths and stories that continue in the present. Our aim as Christian men is, however, more than a mythic quest for lost manhood. We are challenged instead to discover a new vision of humanity for women and men alike grounded in the biblical story.

For men of faith, biblical stories of men have always provided images of manhood. We have been fascinated with the bravery and ingenuity of David when he slew Goliath. The older David's seduction of Bathsheba, however, has unfortunate parallels with the lives of powerful modern men. Many men understand all too well the reluctance to follow God's intent in Jonah's tale. In order to be strong or unique, we may, as Samson did, let our hair grow long. Each of us has a favorite biblical character who mirrors or inspires our struggle to be faithful. Jacob's story has enough ambiguity for all of us. At the same time, the Jacob story is a hopeful sign of transformation. If he had lived as if the past images of being a man were cultural or genetic destiny, Jacob would forever be his mother's trickster and every man's story would already have been defined in the prologue. However, we are living though a gender-role revolution. All bets are off. We are free to respond to the call of the gospel and live beyond our prologue, the stories of our fathers, and the cultural myths of masculinity toward a new vision of faithfulness.

RETHINKING BEING A MAN

The task for men, as writer Susan Faludi has put it, is *not* "to figure out how to be masculine—rather, their masculinity lies in figuring out how to be human."[5] I agree. Men need not be determined by the stories of their fathers or the ancient myths of masculinity. Their nature is neither fixed by testosterone nor confined by culture. Men today have freedom to develop a range of human emotions and practices previously overlooked or underdeveloped. Some of these practices have been underdeveloped in men partly because women did them better and partly because we thought that the activity was more suited to being women than men. So, for example, women are "better" at grieving than men partly because they have had more occasions to grieve as the surviving spouse, but more significantly because we have believed that grieving was more intrinsic to being a woman than being a man. The practice of "stiff-upper-lipping" in grief was more common for men because it was reinforced by other values admired in men such as self-control. In order for men to discover a deeper and fuller sense of their humanity, we need to challenge the presumptions that have divided human activities, like grieving, according to gender and thereby limited the development of certain human qualities in men.

Another aim of this book is to encourage men to explore new ways of being human without hanging on to old scripts of masculinity or rights of ancient privilege. At the same time, we should be cautious about harshly judging men for what they are not. Very often the male practices that need changing are a consequence of other expectations that were once promoted as real masculinity. Because roles and activities for both women and men were socialized according to specific expectations, my presumption is that both women and men will need to develop qualities and skills previously assumed to be gender specific. So, for example, my wife is determined to learn the art of barbecuing, which has previously been in the man's domain. More and more women are balancing ledgers, engaging in military combat, and practicing the weighty art of breadwinning, practices previously limited to the male sphere. On the other side, more and more men are learning to cook, clean toilets, and change diapers. Because we no longer assume that being a man means being the primary provider for a family, it is possible, though not easy, for men to share the responsibility of breadwinning with women as women share cooking and cleaning with men.

> Nowhere is the dynamic of American masculinity more manifest than in our singular contribution to the world's storehouse of cultural heroes: the cowboy. . . . The disappearance of the cowboy as the model of American masculinity will be a gain, not a loss. His disappearance as an individual hero, a template for individual role-modeling, may help free U.S. men from the constraints of a compulsively competitive masculinity and create new options for men as nurturing fathers, expressive husbands and lovers, and generous, sympathetic friends.
>
> Michael S. Kimmel, *Beyond Patriarchy*

This is both an exciting and difficult time to be a man. It is a difficult time because we need to let go of old male models and patterns of interacting that have been part of our self-understanding before we know fully what will take their place. In response to these changes, men often feel vulnerable, off-balance, and bewildered by what Ellis Cose has labeled a "gender-bending time of transition."[6] Men feel powerless and yet women strongly believe that men have all the power. Traditional masculine toughness seems to be out; compassionate gentleness seems to be in. Many men, however, continue to hold the conviction that underneath the sensitive external packaging, women really want a man who will be a rock to stand on and a fortress of protection when the going gets tough. Men seem to be unclear what is expected of them, even though women are generally quite specific how they expect men to change.

Men of all races have an investment in the task of redefining masculinity. However, even when men acknowledge the necessity for change, they are not always pleased with the way things seem to be headed. Black men may not appear to be as upset as white men about the decline of male privilege and power since they had very little to begin with. On the other side, the grief of white males has often been discounted. Some even suggest that male grief for the loss of status and power is trivial and without moral authority because the end of male privilege and dominance is necessary and long overdue. Even so, grief for the necessary loss of privilege is still real grief. If we ignore or invalidate male grief for the loss of dominance or privilege, those feelings will continue to inhibit the intentions of men to embody a new vision of manhood. I believe that being free to grieve the loss of privilege can empower modern men of faith to discover new ways to be manly and faithful.

Developing a new vision of manhood informed by the Christian faith is exciting because men are free to discover new ways of being without the old scripts. The old gender maps are outdated. Efforts to retrieve old patterns of male dominance or privilege are neither possible nor desirable. We are free to redefine what it means to be a man in response to the challenge of the gospel and in the light of the best resources we can find from Scripture, theology, and the human sciences. I hope men will find in this book a positive map for discovering the new possibilities for being human now open to them. This book is about those qualities and practices, common to being human, that have not always been regarded as values internal to being a man. In the process of telling our stories to one another, I hope men will discover aspects of being human that have been overlooked or underdeveloped more by omission than intention.

Prologue

Being a man living toward faithfulness in our time means reclaiming qualities like nurturing, grieving, paying attention, being a friend, sharing power, promising, and acknowledging vulnerability that are common to being human. We begin our exploration with the common experience of disappointment.

HANDLING DISAPPOINTMENT

Isaac was old and his eyes were dim so he could not see. It was time to give the blessing to Esau, the eldest of his twin sons. Rebekah overheard Isaac instructing Esau "to hunt game" and prepare "savory food, such as I like, and bring it to me to eat, so that I may bless you before I die" (Gen. 27:3–4). Rebekah planned the deceit and commanded her favorite son, Jacob, to obey. Rebekah prepared the savory feast, took the best garments of her elder son, Esau, for the charade, and covered the arms and neck of Jacob so that he would appear as a "hairy man." Isaac was not sure it was Esau, but when Isaac smelled the garments of Esau, he blessed Jacob with a blessing he could not take back. David Steele says this about the blessing:

> So be it! The masquerade is over.
> The words are said. There is no taking back.
> Jacob now stands heir to Abram,
> Patriarch of Yahweh.
> He and mother have won.
>
> *And all of this seems a trifle odd*
> *To find within the Word of God.* [1]

Jacob had successfully tricked his father and twin brother to get the blessing that belonged to Esau. However, Jacob did not always get what he wanted, at least not right away. From the first moment that he saw Rachel at the well with her father's sheep, Jacob wanted Rachel to be his wife. "Now when Jacob saw Rachel, the daughter of his mother's brother Laban, and the sheep of his mother's brother Laban, Jacob went up and rolled the stone from the well's mouth, and watered the flock of his mother's brother Laban. Then Jacob kissed Rachel, and wept aloud. . . . Jacob loved Rachel; so he said [to Laban], 'I will serve you seven years for your younger daughter Rachel'" (Gen. 29:10–11, 18). Laban agreed and Jacob served his uncle for seven years to gain marriage to Rachel.

When Jacob had fulfilled his part of the agreement, Jacob asked his uncle Laban for Rachel as his wife. Laban deceived Jacob and instead of Rachel brought his older daughter, Leah, to the nuptial meeting. Obviously, a little light on the wedding night would have made Laban's deception impossible. It was not right, Laban explained in the morning's light when Jacob realized he had been tricked, for a younger sister to precede her older sister in marriage. Laban's pretense of politeness and family solidarity turned into a cunning scheme to insure that both his daughters would be married. Because Jacob loved Rachel more than Leah, he swallowed his anger, managed his disappointment, and served Laban for seven more years in order to marry Rachel as well. Jacob had many sons and one daughter with Leah but for a long time no children with Rachel. It was another disappointment. Finally, Rachel had two sons: Joseph and then Benjamin. Because of Jacob's love for Rachel, these two sons were his favorites.

After Joseph's birth, Jacob wanted to go back to his home country. Laban was aware, however, that he had been blessed by Jacob's presence and so he discouraged Jacob from leaving. Jacob agreed to continue to work for Laban. In return, Jacob was to receive in payment all the newborn striped or speckled goats and lambs. Laban was delighted with the agreement and immediately violated the spirit of the contract by removing all the grown animals that would be likely to produce spotted or striped offspring. This time, Jacob managed his disappointment by outwitting his father-in-law through visual aids at the watering places where the flocks bred. The trickery worked and "the flocks produced young that were striped, speckled, and spotted" (Gen. 30:39). It was yet another instance in which Jacob got what he wanted by deception, although this time the animals were deceived. His time in Haran with his mother's brother Laban had been twenty years of disappointment for Jacob. Along the way, Laban changed Jacob's wages ten times. Jacob was deceived as he had deceived. Even so, Jacob endured because God was with him through all his disappointments.

At the end of Jacob's life, when Joseph introduced his father to Pharaoh, the ruler of Egypt asked Jacob his age. It is presumed that Pharaoh asked this question because Jacob seemed older than his years. Jacob's answer confirmed that interpretation of the question. "The years of my earthly sojourn are one hundred thirty; few and hard have been the years of my life" (Gen. 47:9). His life did not turn out as he dreamed it would when he brazenly stole his father's blessing. The end of his life was filled with bitter memories of unfulfilled dreams and unmet expectations.

It is impossible to live without disappointment. Children are disappointed when they do not find what they want for Christmas under the tree. Even when they get what they want, children may have that crestfallen look because the gift is the wrong brand or color or not the up-to-date version. Not getting picked to play on the best midget hockey team or not being chosen to be a school-crossing guard are other early moments of disappointment. Not being accepted by the best college, making the honor roll, being picked for the wrestling team, being elected class president, or winning the lottery are experiences in which hopes are shattered or expectations are frustrated and we are disappointed. The woman of our dreams may marry someone else. The dream of a picture-perfect marriage may be shattered by divorce. The job promotion we wanted and worked hard to achieve may go to a friend who does not want it. Disappointment is a common human experience.

We are disappointed when our parents break promises or our children do not meet our expectations. We are also disappointed when friends deceive us or neighbors take advantage of us. If we conclude at the end of a life that it did not turn out like we hoped it would, the disappointment may be intense and enduring. It is difficult to live with the pain of disappointment. Generally, men do not handle disappointment well. With a stiff upper lip, we change the subject, pretend it didn't matter anyway, walk away in silence, or hide in shame. Because it is such a common experience, however, learning how to handle disappointment is an important life task for men as they seek to discover new dimensions of being human.

WHAT IS DISAPPOINTMENT?

Disappointment occurs when we fail to fulfill our expectations or satisfy our dreams. Whether those expectations are thwarted by others, impeded by happenstance, or frustrated by our own foolish actions, we are profoundly sad and even a little angry when things do not go as planned. If no one knew about the dream that did not materialize, the pain might be kept private. If the setback is public, however, the disappointment may include shame and humiliation. In order to maintain our image or save face in the community, disappointment is often covered by pretense or deception. Disappointment may not be as intense or prolonged as grief or as demoralizing as depression and despair, but the pain is nonetheless real whenever hopes are dashed.

While writing this chapter, I had a phone conversation with the widow of a dear friend. The story of Paul's dying put disappointment in perspective. Paul's wife had been thinking how disappointed her husband had been about dying just at the point when all the things he valued and had worked to accomplish were within grasp. It would have been easier for Paul, she said, if he had died five years earlier when his work situation was more ambiguous. Before the conversation ended, we both agreed that what Paul experienced in the last week of his life was more than disappointment: it was a devastation. In the span of a week, he went from being a gentle Christian man praying for strength to enter the mystery of dying to a speechless person terrified of being alone. It was a devastating, sometimes frightening struggle with unseen angels who came to bring him home to God. In the midst of that anguish, he reached out one of his trembling arms and made the sign of the cross on a friend's forehead. Paul was at peace in the promise that the cross of Christ transforms all human disappointment.

There are times, like Paul's dying, when disappointment does not convey the tragic character of an experience. Words like destruction and devastation seem more appropriate. The emotional pain of disappointment is real, however, even if it does not compare with the devastation of dying like Paul, losing a lifetime of work in a fire, or ending a marriage that you thought would last forever. Disappointment is common in human life but it is not everything. Having said that, we need to remind one another that suffering is always in the eyes of the beholder. One man's disappointment is another man's devastation. For that reason, we need to be empathic with ourselves and other men without judging the source of disappointment.

DISAPPOINTMENT BECAUSE OF THE LOSS OF DREAMS

One source of deep disappointment is the shattering of dreams of what one might become or how life might be. Dreams are fashioned over time as we come to understand what we want and hope for in life. When we invest emotionally in these dreams or expectations, they become visions of the future that *must* occur for life to be fulfilled. The key is emotional investment. The poet Langston Hughes has aptly described a world without dreams as a "barren field, frozen with snow."[2] Our dreams give shape to hope and direction to strategic planning. They give life to barren lives. The loss of dreams refers to inner experiences when our expectations about life are no longer possible. The loss of dreams is a kind of *intraphysic loss* that I once defined as "losing the possibilities of 'what might have been,' abandonment of plans for a particular future, and the dying of a dream." Our dreams become so much a part of our identity it is not surprising that shattered dreams deplete the self.

In a useful little book, *The Loss of Dreams: A Special Kind of Grief*, Ted Bowman has developed the idea of intrapsychic loss primarily around the loss of dreams. "A loss of dreams relates to images or pictures of our personal world that we create and to which we attach strong emotional investment . . . the way things are supposed to be."[3] Ten-year-old boys on the back streets of Chicago or Detroit dream of being professional basketball stars. Fathers have dreams for their children that children may reject or that are shattered by a knee injury in the last high school football game or an arrest for drug possession. For some men, the dreams they have for themselves are not about achievement but security, good health, happiness, or a vision of a world at peace. The power of a dream is that it focuses our passions and disciplines our energy.

Because our dreams are very personal and fragile, they are often privately kept. We may not even know the dreams we hold until we note their passing. For that reason, the intensity of disappointment is often unpredictable. The story of Kevin illustrates the private pain of the private loss of a very private dream. Kevin had set as a personal goal to be the Midwest regional sales manager for a muffler company by the age of forty. When he was forty-two and it was clear that he would never be a regional manager, Kevin committed suicide. Only his secretary knew why because she was the only person who knew his dream. His life was shattered when he realized his dream of being a regional manager would not be fulfilled. Kevin's future hinged on fulfilling the dream. He could not imagine living with the disappointment. Although the endings may not always be as tragic as Kevin's, the death of a dream is a story often repeated, frequently unknown, and always devastating.

Sometimes the dream is so private we do not even recognize the loss that has occurred within us. Our focus is so clearly on the goal ahead or the tasks before us that we are inattentive to internal loss and sadness. Or perhaps the disappointment or sadness is hidden behind over-achieving activities. I have a friend who was given a prestigious position at the school where he teaches. My hunch is that the promotion is more of a burden than an honor, complicated by his internal expectations of holding this prestigious position. He is fearful of being a disappointment to others. He works all the time and over prepares but I suspect he still worries whether his work is good enough to hold the position. Along the way, his anxiety has shut him off from some close friends. I am sure my friend would not recognize himself in my description of his internal struggle. Men are particularly unwilling to acknowledge internal loss or disappointment when it is connected to an honor, a promotion, or a new responsibility that takes us out of our personal comfort zone. Rather than admit we are unsure or afraid, we fake it.

Because the dreams are secret, the grief is hidden. So it was with Kevin and so it is with many men. It is important that we pay particular attention to the loss of dreams among the young. Too many young men are trapped in cycles of poverty or racial abuse and see no hope for the future. For them, every tomorrow seems bleak and without hope. Even for young men of privilege, the options are fewer than they generally were for their parents. They still dream but there is less certainty that the dreams will be realized. The cynicism and apathy that one hears from young people are born out of the realization that their prospects are limited. Because fathers are vaguely uncomfortable about creating a future more limited than the one they inherited, they are reluctant to talk with their sons and so create a conspiracy of silence around the future.

The loss of dreams is a major moment for men in the middle of their lives. When there is more time behind than ahead, men reluctantly but almost inevitably begin to make an assessment of their lives. The novelist James Baldwin described midlife in this way. "Between what one wishes to become and what one has become there is a *momentous gap*, which will now never be closed. And this gap seems to operate as one's final margin, one's last opportunity for creation."[4] The discontinuity between this inner landscape and outer terrain is often the occasion for melancholy or sadness muted only by the intense desire to retain the appearance of personal continuity or perennial youthfulness. Rather than facing finitude directly, men will engage in behavior we label "a midlife crisis" designed to diminish the pain of loss. Most of the time, we feel good about what has been accomplished. Sometimes, however, these moments in midlife are the occasion for deep disappointment because we become aware that things in our lives are not as they could have been or we wish they were. This gap between dreams and reality is one reason men fear incompleteness as much as death. It is also why men are reluctant to talk to their sons about a limited future.

DISAPPOINTMENT AND DECEPTION

The deception that dominated Jacob's life fostered the likelihood of more disappointment. He was deceived as he deceived. It is a pattern that too many men understand. When pretense and deception become a common life pattern, promises are easily broken, trust is diminished, and ordinary human bonds that are necessary to achieve our hopes and dreams are broken. All reality is virtual. Jacob did not tell his uncle Laban that he was leaving Haran to return to his home country. Unfortunately, like Jacob, we too may presume that deception is the only way to handle deep disappointment with a workplace. Even when we would like to tell the company the working conditions are unsatisfactory, we choose instead to leave secretly to accept a position with a rival firm. As they left Haran, Rachel deceived Jacob and secretly took her father Laban's household gods to insure that Jacob would get his rightful share of the inheritance. Modern men understand Jacob's anger. The deception that is most painful comes from those we love the most.

When Laban learned that Jacob had vanished, taking away his daughters and his grandchildren and threatening the good fortune that Jacob had produced, he went in pursuit. On the way, he was warned in a dream to beware of attempting anything with Jacob, "good or bad" (Gen. 31:24). It is a kind of truce we often come to when we have been frequently deceived and disappointed and coexistence is the best we can hope for. In order to insure the truce, Laban and Jacob made a pledge that ironically has become a treasured benediction for people who must be separated. "The LORD watch between you and me, when we are absent one from another" (Gen. 31:49). David Steele captures the irony of the pledge.

This is no expression of peace and solidarity
By men whose hands are clasped in faith.
It is the call of men who hold suspicions
Upon the God of Vengeance
To be policeman in their parting.
So once again, our hero gets
To leave a place midst angry threats.
My, Jacob surely has the knack
Of causing folks to blow their stack! 5

Jacob's life describes what most men know painfully well: deception feeds on itself and generates more deception. Before we know what has happened, we are caught in a web of lies and pretense so that (1) we are no longer certain what is true and (2) we are sure to be disappointed when we look for affection or love.

Because we are finite creatures, it is not really possible to live without disappointment or regret. There will always be something more we could have done or should have done or would have done if only we had more courage, better luck, or more enduring trust in the goodness of God who holds the future. Sharing disappointments or regret honestly not only makes intimacy possible; it builds character. Honesty transforms eyes of pretense into windows of trust. We see that our achievements are finite but so are our failures. Our lives are finally judged according to limited possibilities. We are free to live in the confidence that God who ordained the boundaries of life will accept our finite completeness. Seeing failure and success through the lens of finite completeness is one strategy men need to learn to cope with disappointment.

STRATEGIES FOR DEALING EFFECTIVELY WITH DISAPPOINTMENT

Acknowledge the loss. The first task is to admit to ourselves and to others that we have been disappointed or have disappointed ourselves. Another way to say this is that honesty is a key to handling disappointment effectively. It is still difficult for men to be honest about failure, disappointment, or even a minor mistake that could damage a public image of competence and control. The expectation that men must be strong and present a winning image makes admitting or acknowledging loss always risky. This is another illustration of unacceptable male behavior (handling disappointment through deception) that is the dark side of positive male behavior (being in charge and presenting an image of competence). While there is no particular virtue in public exposure of human failing, the need to promote a successful self-image has sometimes led to seriously damaging patterns of self-deception and pretense in men. Authenticity in human interaction is one way of describing a new way of being a man that combines honesty with strength.

Until the loss is acknowledged or the disappointment noted, the healing process cannot begin. In the meantime, unexpressed hurt, anger, or shame connected to a job loss or financial setback hidden by deception will aggravate the original loss. It was two months before Dan was able to tell his wife that he had been let go by his company. He left for work and came home at the same time as he had done before. During the day he drank coffee, read the paper, and answered ads from his cell phone. To be sure that no one would suspect he was out of work, he developed a two-week cycle of ten coffee shops where he did his "work." At the end of the six weeks, he still did not have a job and his severance pay ended. When the money ran out, Dan's wife, Lisa, finally learned that he had lost his job two months before. She could share his disappointment but the deception diminished her trust of Dan when he needed it most. When men feel they need to cover their disappointment as Dan did, they turn away human resources for living through the pain.

Grieve the loss. Once named, shattered dreams must be grieved. There is no comfort in hiding from grief, whenever it occurs. Many types of loss may accompany disappointment—the loss of relationships, the loss of dreams, the loss of role or status that work provides, the loss of identity and purpose. Sometimes the loss that leads to disappointment also generates a sense of disenchantment, an experience of misplaced trust, or the feeling of betrayal. Even if the loss is internal, the grief needs to be expressed externally. That process of grieving may include letting go of outdated images of ourselves that keep setting us up for disappointment.

The story of Dan and Lisa illustrates how important it is to develop a strategy for dealing with disappointment so that deception does not compound the pain. Healing begins with acknowledging the loss. In a later chapter on grieving, we will explore how important it is for men to create safe places to express their grief. Too often, men feel they must hide their disappointment in the church as well. Helping men to handle their disappointment without hiding their shame is another significant ministry a congregation could provide. While fixing the roof or raising money to support young people preparing for ministry in the church are important tasks to do, making a safe place in the church for men to share their heartaches without fear is an essential ministry of our time.

Forgive those who thwart the dream. If the disappointed griever is always a victim, it is difficult to acknowledge responsibility for the loss that has occurred. There is a tendency in this society to look for someone to blame for our losses. Seeking revenge for the loss of a dream is unfortunately so common in this society that we have coined a term for it: "going postal." People "go postal" when they feel so powerless and angry because of downsizing that they kill people who they believe are responsible for their plight. Mark O. Barton is the day trader who killed three people from places where he had worked. In his suicide note, Mark wrote of his wife that he "killed Leigh Ann because she was one of the main reasons for my demise."[6] Mark was very clear who he thought caused his failure. When the sources of our disappointment are not visible, however, we may invent enemies, people or institutions we believe prevented us from achieving our expectations.

Imagine new possibilities. When we have been disappointed, it is difficult to dream about a new future. When a marriage ends, when a son dies of AIDS, when the new corporate management makes drastic changes that diminish the value of work, when it seems that God is far away, it is easy to stop dreaming. When we stop dreaming, we stop living fully. The tragedy in life is not that expectations are unmet or dreams unfulfilled but that we stop dreaming. Sometimes in order to imagine new possibilities or dream again, we need to modify or let go of particular visions for the future. Letting go of dreams is a loss one must grieve. That process of grieving may include letting go of outdated images of ourselves or unrealistic expectations of others that keep setting us up for disappointment.

SHAKE THE DUST FROM YOUR SANDALS: DISAPPOINTMENT WITHOUT CYNICISM

Most of the time, we choose to endure disappointments and start over. Sometimes, however, we get trapped in a seemingly endless cycle of setbacks that turn life sour. The chief enemy of the soul is not disappointment or sadness but pretense and cynicism. We have seen in the story of Jacob how deception feeds on itself and promotes more disappointment. When disappointments are not resolved, they fester and foster a negative attitude about life that tilts toward cynicism. If the personal return on our emotional investment in the company, our marriage, or the church men's group is not enough, the temptation is to withdraw, shut down, declare it was a dumb idea in the first place, pledge not to do it again, and risk becoming cynical. When we conclude that nobody really cares, nothing matters, people cannot be trusted, change is not possible, and no matter how hard we try, things are not likely to get better, then disappointment has turned to cynicism.

The ministry of Jesus provides an alternative for handling disappointment without cynicism that is at once simple and complex. In his instruction to the disciples before they were sent on mission, Jesus said: "If anyone will not welcome you or listen to your words, shake off the dust from your feet as you leave that house or town" (Matt. 10:14). The advice is simple. When you are disappointed or things don't go your way, let it go. Do not take any dust particles with you, suggests Jesus. When we tell a friend who is pushing a losing cause, belaboring a rejection, or insisting on getting even to "give it up," the advice is similar. Once we have named the pain and grieved the loss, we need to let go of the disappointment in order to dream again and move toward a new future. It is not easy for men to lose or let go. "Giving it up" seems too much like defeat but it is the only healing option. Disappointment will not go away on its own accord. We need to grieve the loss and let it go, believing that God will make a new future.

The future that God will make new is a mystery. We will have dreams and expectations for tomorrow but they need to be provisional in the light of faith. One of the characteristics of Christian faithfulness is to make dreams for the future without investing in the outcome of those dreams. The outcome belongs to God who continues to work quietly and mysteriously through us to reweave the web of life. Along the way there will be disappointments. People will let us down and we will let ourselves down. Some of our noble risks will fail. Some little efforts will succeed. Even so, we do all we can to make a better world, not knowing whether any of it is right, not knowing whether what we do will make a difference, but believing that God's purposes will be fulfilled in God's time and in God's way. What keeps us going is the conviction that what we do has meaning and purpose in the providence of God.

ACKNOWLEDGING VULNERABILITY

Jacob won his father's blessing by deception but lost his home. "Your brother Esau is consoling himself by planning to kill you," Rebekah warned Jacob (Gen. 27:42). As Jacob left, his father added another blessing to insure that Jacob would marry one of Laban's daughters instead of a Canaanite woman. Deception continued to be part of Jacob's life. This time, however, he was on the receiving end. Although his uncle Laban deceived him on numerous occasions, Jacob prospered and became rich with sheep and cattle. Even so, Jacob was in a vulnerable spot because his cousins resented his wealth. When Jacob realized that Laban also no longer regarded him favorably, Jacob was caught between a rock and a hard place: between the hostility with Laban and sons in Haran and his lingering fear of Esau's revenge at home. Jacob determined to flee from Haran with his wives and possessions to go to his father in the land of Canaan, which also meant going toward Esau.

Jacob still feared Esau. On the way to Canaan he prayed that God would deliver him from the hand of Esau, "for I am afraid of him; he may come and kill us all, the mothers with the children" (Gen. 32:11). Because of his fear of Esau, Jacob sent ahead wave upon wave of animals as gifts, and wives and children as protection. Jacob would follow. The night before he met Esau, Jacob wrestled with an angel of God until daybreak in search of another blessing and security to settle his fear. As often happens, the encounter with God cost Jacob more than he anticipated: his hip was put out of joint and he got a new name—Israel. David Steele has captured Jacob's vulnerability with this verse:

> So Jacob, master wheeler dealer
> Is Israel, the wounded healer.
> And we among the human throng
> Are called to come and limp along.[1]

And so Jacob limped to the feared encounter with his brother Esau, now without either terror or bravado. He had seen God face to face and his life had been preserved. Once again, Jacob had an experience of God's graciousness. Ironically, recognizing his vulnerability made Jacob better prepared for his dreaded encounter with Esau. This time Jacob hung on to God, driven by the desperation of his own weakness rather than struggle against God with his own strength. The presence of physical vulnerability was a sign to Jacob that his future did not depend on power or cunning deception but on God's providence.

Being vulnerable is part of being human. Without fangs or claws, without fur or venom, the human creature is born dependent and susceptible to being wounded. As a result, humans need care and protection at the beginning of life much longer than other creatures. Eventually, humans make tools and weapons for protection in order to survive without built-in armor. We also develop character armor to protect our person from emotional injury or to avoid thinking about death. Even a young child who moves about independently is not self-sufficient without language to communicate needs and desires. Sometimes children are wounded rather than protected. Those memories of childhood injury or abuse prompt adults to develop life patterns that aim to diminish vulnerability.

Even when they have no memories of being wounded, men are still inclined to think about overcoming the dependence and vulnerability of childhood as the aim of growing up. Invulnerability is assumed to be a fundamental characteristic of manliness. In order to support this masculine fantasy, men strut and swagger and give the appearance of invulnerability when they feel attacked. Because it has been a pattern for so long, men have little practice acknowledging vulnerability. Because the inability to live with vulnerability is common among men, it is not surprising that men also struggle with emotional intimacy and friendship. Maintaining friendship presupposes a willingness to be known by another. The reluctance to acknowledge vulnerability also helps explain why there are usually more women than men in church. Belonging to a church is recognition that men need community in order to live with vulnerability.

SUSCEPTIBILITY TO BEING WOUNDED

Being vulnerable simply means that we are susceptible to being physically injured or emotionally wounded. Vulnerability quite literally means "susceptible to being wounded." It is not something we can avoid. It is part of being human. No one is invulnerable. All human beings are susceptible to wounding because we are finite creatures who get sick and die. We are particularly susceptible to being wounded when we are isolated and lonely or when we are powerless and afraid. We may also feel vulnerable when more information, stimuli, or expectations are coming at us than we can manage or ignore. Invulnerability is not only a human impossibility, it is an undesirable quality. Acknowledging vulnerability is a reminder to men that we cannot make it alone without the presence of God in our lives. If we are lucky enough to have a limp of some kind, an obvious impediment like stuttering or poor eyesight, we are personally aware, and so are others, of both dependence and vulnerability.

Jacob's life of deception intensified his ordinary human vulnerability. Whenever we fabricate lies or distort the truth, we increase the possibility of being attacked or injured. That is a human reality. We are, for example, more vulnerable to manipulation when portions of our lives must be hidden. The fear of Esau that kept him from returning home is mirrored in the ways that men must hide because they are fearful of being known. The struggle against Esau had been part of Jacob's life since before his birth. In his wrestling with an angel, Jacob worked through his guilt for deceiving Esau and his terror of meeting him. Jacob awoke from his dream convinced that he had faced his struggle with courage and been blessed. Having seen God face to face, Jacob could then prepare to meet Esau face to face. The limp Jacob got on his way to the encounter with Esau was a tangible reminder to Jacob that his future did not depend on his power or cunning but in God's providence. Again, David Steele captures the vulnerability of Jacob, a limping wrestler, who now walks toward his brother with empty hands.

> It's quite a shock to see this new man
> Limping into his tomorrow.
> His hands are empty.
> No bags of gold; no rabbit up his sleeve,
> Empty hands . . .
> As empty as on the day when he was born . . .
> No, emptier . . . for they hold no brother's heel.
> He has no schemes nor scams.
> It's strange, but he can't seem to recall
> His mother's words that once seemed so important.
> (Wasn't it something about winning?)
> He limps now and will to his dying day.
> And in that limp conveys to all
> That he has shared the pain of our mortality.
> (Never trust a patriarch without a limp.)[2]

This chapter explores the theme of vulnerability in men in a variety of ways. It is not an easy exploration to make, for most men resist acknowledging that because they are human, they are susceptible to being wounded. We do not want a competitor to know that we have any weakness or windows of vulnerability that might be used against us. We are taught to watch our flank or cover our behind. Even being understood is regarded as dangerous for some because people may use what they know about us to their advantage. The story of Jacob wrestling through the night in anticipation of a feared meeting is a familiar story. For us the feared meeting may be an annual review with a boss, a reunion with an estranged son, or a long-postponed conversation about the future of a marriage. We may wrestle with an unnamed stranger in a dream or with fitful waking and sleeping through the night. If in the morning we have found resolution and peace from the struggle, it will usually mean that we have acknowledged vulnerability in a new way and we are less afraid.

A Particular Vulnerability

The diagnosis of prostate was stunning news. Since I have never been very good at faking, I decided very soon to tell everyone I knew that I had cancer. Some well-meaning friends sought to mollify my initial worry by insisting that prostate cancer is not as serious as other forms of cancer, especially if, as in my case, it is detected early and treated aggressively. I gently reminded those people that having cancer is a little like being pregnant: you are or you are not. For others, the mention of cancer was a death sentence. Their alarm produced some fear in me that I had not taken my diagnosis seriously enough. Others were awkward about my honesty and changed the subject. Because men regard prostate cancer as a private battle that diminishes manliness, no one should speak of it. Because many men have had difficulty speaking openly about prostate cancer, loneliness is frequently added to the fear of death or the loss of virility. Although the prostate is well hidden in the body, prostate cancer need not and should not be a secret. For me, the benefit of not keeping the diagnosis of prostate cancer a secret is that I have been sustained by the well wishes and prayers of many people from all around the globe. That great company of compassion has been for me a gracious gift.

From very early in the diagnosis, I have been surprisingly peaceful about having prostate cancer. Because I am a world-class worrier, that peacefulness was somewhat surprising to me and to my family. So I worried for a while about not worrying. I wondered whether I was denying the seriousness of the illness or ducking my fear of death. And then a friend quietly reminded me that I have spent twenty-five years teaching about death. In particular, I have tried to convey through both writing and teaching a simple truth that is consistent with the Christian faith but which I learned most clearly from the writing of Ernest Becker: in order to deny the inevitability of death and the reality of finitude, people promote heroism and fashion character armor that ultimately cuts them off from life and they die before they are dead. I believe what I have taught. Human beings are finite, contingent, vulnerable creatures. Death is the final expression of human finitude and there is no escape. So, in a strange sense, I am peaceful about being diagnosed with prostate cancer because it is documentation of what I have long suspected: I am a finite, contingent creature in God's care. I cannot hide from my vulnerability.

There is a certain irony in writing a book about men while experiencing prostate cancer. On the one hand, the primary purpose of the prostate is to produce a thick fluid that forms part of semen, which men frequently connect with masculine power or potency. Because treatment for prostate cancer sometimes diminishes the capacity for an erection, it is often difficult for men to speak of an illness that touches so close to the presumed locus of potency and male identity. On the other hand, the prostate is not only the presumed source of masculinity: it is the physical place in the male body most susceptible to cancer. Some medical researchers have speculated that if every male over sixty-five had a biopsy, one in four would have prostate cancer. What is certain is about 200,000 men are diagnosed with cancer of the prostate each year. Having prostate cancer is tangible evidence that men *are* susceptible to being wounded at the locus of sexual power.

BALANCING POWER AND VULNERABILITY

This close connection between potency or power and vulnerability in male anatomy is a metaphor about what men need to learn about being human. Except perhaps for the act of bearing children, women have been perceived to be powerless, or even helpless, needing male power for protection. Even when women have gained personal and social power, they still live with a constant consciousness of their physical and sexual vulnerability. By contrast, men have generally presumed power without susceptibility to wounding. Prostate cancer is emotionally unsettling for men precisely because we are vulnerable at the source of our potency. Whenever men presume to be invulnerable in the exercise of power, it is easy to treat with disdain what cannot wound us. Invulnerability also prompts self-sufficiency and isolation. Learning to acknowledge vulnerability will not lead necessarily to impotence if it is balanced with an appropriate sense of power. I believe that the lives of men would be enhanced and society would be safer if men lived with a greater awareness of the close link between power and vulnerability.

The *preemptive strike in the face of loss* is another useful way to avoid feeling too exposed and needy in close relationships. Often, when men feel in danger of being humiliated by women or other men, they will attempt to strike the first blow, thus forestalling their own vulnerability. . . . We [also] learn about the heroism of male achievement and authority, but not about the heroism of male vulnerability and uncertainty, and how to live without having all the answers.

Sam Osherson, *Wrestling with Love: How Men Struggle with Intimacy with Women, Children, Parents, and Each Other*

Although I have always felt vulnerable, I was usually unsuccessful in convincing others of that reality. I did not look or act vulnerable. I was the strong one that people leaned on when they felt vulnerable. Now, however, I have proof I was right all along. I have prostate cancer. I am susceptible to being wounded. Once I made that discovery, I understood why I told people I hardly knew that I had prostate cancer. It is difficult for men to live with the conviction that power and vulnerability are twin companions of every human soul. We are, in fact, most powerful when we are most vulnerable and most vulnerable at the height of our power. If men could understand this deep connection between power and vulnerability, we might be less terrified by either one.

Cancer is only one dramatic sign that human beings are vulnerable to attack from forces outside our control. Environments in which we live are full of contaminants that threaten our physical health and emotional well-being. I have told this story from my life because I believe that the inability to acknowledge vulnerability is a major impediment for men who want to discover their full humanity. The presumption that we can construct an invulnerable life is a dangerous myth because it impedes full living. Gated communities and elaborate security systems are only two instances of efforts to create places of safety invulnerable to attack. Although human ingenuity continues to search for danger-free havens or a permanent summer resort far from the madding crowds, we know that such havens are a romantic illusion. We will stand and fall together, not because we are walled off from one another in secure enclaves but because we have learned to live with contingency and we have created communities of vulnerable ones.

VULNERABLE MOMENTS FOR MEN

Vulnerability, we have already said, is part of the human condition. It is also something that men in particular seek to avoid. When we say that a man is vulnerable to this or that, we suggest something about his susceptibility to a positive or negative influence. Vulnerability comes from within and from without. Consider Sam's story. He is fifty-nine years old, employed at General Motors, where he expects to work until sixty-five. He has been in good health except for an occasional heart arrhythmia and a recently elevated PSA (prostate specific antigen). The biopsy that followed was positive but the recommended treatment is *watchful waiting.* "I have told few people about either my heart condition or my prostate," he said, "principally due to fear in the workplace that I will be stereotyped. I am considered an excellent worker in every respect and I want to keep that perception. I do not want them to perceive me as weak or unable to do my work. My masculinity is at stake here." Sam's heart arrhythmia and his prostate condition are concrete signs of vulnerability even though they are not visible, but his desire to hide those ailments in order not to jeopardize his status in the workplace is the result of internal fears that exaggerate his experience of vulnerability. We bring a variety of emotional conditions to any situation that will increase or decrease the dangerousness of susceptibility. There are also particular situations that are more likely to intensify ordinary human vulnerability.

Men experience vulnerability when they fail to perform as expected. Failure to perform sexually is one of the most painful experiences of vulnerability for men. What makes those moments particularly painful is being exposed as powerless. Even if our sexual partner assures us that our inability to perform is not what matters, we will judge ourselves by internalized performance expectations of manhood. There are other circumstances when our inability to perform heightens our awareness of being vulnerable creatures. Boys have been known to hide a bad report card until father goes on a business trip. A rejection from the college of choice is often a shameful failure. A performance review at work usually generates some anxiety. If it leads to dismissal, the inability to handle disappointment or failure because of an inability to acknowledge vulnerability may lead to rage over powerlessness or hidden despair.

Men feel vulnerable when their role or status is undermined. The positions we hold or the roles we fulfill are like a cloak men wear: we feel protected from surprise or from powerlessness by status we have achieved or roles we have been assigned. Being without a role or status seems too much like being naked and vulnerable, especially for men who are accustomed to being protected by their roles or position. When men "pull rank" in a crisis or when they are attacked, it is a way of using role or status to eliminate ambiguity or resolve conflict. The question "Who's in charge here?" is intended to settle matters. The difficulty with this method of coping is that it perpetuates itself. Because men have had the power positions for so long, it is easy for men to fall back on role or rank when they feel vulnerable. Men hang on to status under threat even when they want to work for greater equality because it is how men cope when things are out of hand. One of the critical agendas for men today is to develop constructive, alternative strategies for handling crisis, conflict, or diminishment without status props. This theme is explored further in the chapter about sharing power.

Men are vulnerable when they are demoralized. There is, I believe, a connection between morale and morals. Demoralization is a precondition for unethical behavior. It occurs when unmet needs determine and even justify our action. Sexual misconduct in the workplace may simply be an abuse of power. It may also be precipitated by an inability to address loneliness or despair in ministry in a constructive and appropriate manner. A friend of mine said it this way not so long ago: "I am aware of vulnerability but always it seems I become aware of particular dangers when it is nearly too late." He is not alone. If men can know that they are vulnerable and how they are vulnerable, they can take precautions before it is too late. Sometimes demoralization sets in before we can know it. For that reason, we need friends to hear our story, keep us honest, and hold us when we hurt.

Men feel vulnerable when they are wrong or perceived to be weak. On this matter, it is perception that matters. What is most important is to give the impression of strength or competence. Men try not to show weakness of any kind. Strength is safety. Weakness is dangerous because one becomes vulnerable to attack. It is weakness to show grief or not know how to do something. For some men, it is a sign of weakness to be wrong or humiliated. For many men simply asking for directions if one is lost is more humiliating than they can bear. They would rather get lost or run out of gas than admit they don't know the way. Being wrong is another form of humiliation. In order to prop men up, many women in the past have been willing to play a charade in which father always knows best and men are right. That pattern trapped both women and men in a negative cycle that diminishes the strength of women and covers over the vulnerability of men.

Men are particularly vulnerable when the work they do is available for public scrutiny. Teachers, performers of any kind, athletes, ministers, and political figures are susceptible to being wounded by criticism, personal attack, or false accusations. Men who have developed a controlled exterior may not reveal woundedness even when they feel it. Doug Purnell, whose art appears throughout this book, wrote recently about the particular vulnerability of an artist. "As artist," Doug wrote, "I express deeper things of my soul in a voice that is beyond normal speech. Then with courage, I hang the work on the wall. I deliberately use the word courage because my ego is vulnerable; it takes a beating when there is no response from some and insensitive responses from others." If the work we do makes a soul visible, it matters greatly that we have attended to the vitality of the soul and the congruence of the self. Fostering authenticity will diminish the pain of criticism but it will strengthen our courage to embody vulnerability.

LIVING WITH VULNERABILITY

While it is possible that we may choose to minimize risk in our lives, we cannot avoid vulnerability. We are more likely to get into difficulty when we hide our vulnerability behind a cloak of control or a carefully constructed public persona that promotes an image of men detrimental to human wholeness. In order to live with an awareness of our vulnerability, we need to find ways to protect ourselves from being overwhelmed by the suffering that often comes with being vulnerable.

It should not be surprising, if we understand the desire for dominance and invulnerability among men, that men are not drawn to the image of Jesus as the vulnerability of God. When men say that church is for women and children, they are admitting that belief in God requires acknowledging human vulnerability. David Steele makes an engaging connection between Jacob's limp and Jesus.

> Jacob limps into history.
> And later on some folks will notice
> A man, carrying a burden,
> Toward a hill called Golgotha.
> His walk will be distinctive.
> And folks will say to one another:
> "Say . . . that one limps . . . just like Israel."[3]

The manly ideal, Dorothee Soelle has observed, is opposed by the Crucified Christ. "The masculine myth of the invulnerable hero is opposed to the unarmed carpenter's son from Galilee: there is nothing here to harmonize."[4] We need a window of vulnerability if we are to live with Christ as God's wound in the world. There are approaches to the Christian faith that emphasize invulnerability and success as signs of God's presence. They are false promises that can only be sustained by also denying the abundance of suffering in the world as signs of God's vulnerability. The idol of invulnerability in the name of security also keeps many men from genuine intimacy or the appropriate exercise of power.

What is at stake in living with vulnerability is hope that endures. New Testament scholar J. Christiaan Beker once observed that hope not connected to human suffering has no ground and may become blind fate. If we are overwhelmed by uncertainty, terror, and hopelessness in the world, it is easy to become either cynical or succumb to sectarian preachers who impose their timetable of futures on the present. "We repress hope and become cynics or we repress suffering and become credulous ideologues."[5] The more correspondence there is between our personal vulnerability and the world's suffering, the easier it is to be overwhelmed by vulnerability. The global scope of suffering seems to exacerbate the intensity with which we experience suffering in our personal lives, so as to add fresh power to the mood of fear that drives us to seek security and avoid vulnerability.

PRACTICING VULNERABILITY

It is unlikely that we can deepen our ability to acknowledge vulnerability as men unless we risk new behavior. My assumption throughout this book is that men have underdeveloped or unpracticed human qualities that we need to address in order to maximize our full human potential. Those qualities are often the other side of masculine qualities or male behaviors that have been encouraged in men, like being the "invulnerable strong one." Men may be motivated to embrace new dimensions of being human by new insight and understanding, or new insight into our humanity as men may follow from acting differently. Reading this book may invite new understanding and insight about being a man. However, sometimes the transforming insight comes only after we risk new behavior. Here are some suggestions for practicing vulnerability.

- *Take the initiative to tell a friend how much the friendship means.* You might even acknowledge that you need his or her friendship because it fills you up when you are empty or opens up your world when you want to shut it down.

- *Admit you are wrong once a week.* This may be difficult for people who are in fact always right, but with a little effort it is usually possible to find some moment when we have made a minor misjudgment.

- *Attend church.* I suspect that men who have difficulty acknowledging vulnerability will avoid attending church as well because being part of a Christian community reminds us of our neediness.

- *Express a deep feeling of hurt or sadness to a close friend.* As much as anything, men need to acknowledge to themselves where they are susceptible to being wounded. We may need to begin by crying alone.

- *Be willing to admit being needy once a week.* When theologian Arthur McGill described the Christian life as "resting in neediness," he presented a challenge for everyone, and perhaps men especially, who has difficulty needing someone else. "In the kingdom of Jesus, however, in the new kind of identity which he brings, where we are constantly receiving and never holding and possessing, . . . here human life is a *resting-in-neediness*."6 Of all the marks of Christian faithfulness, this may be the most difficult challenge for men. For that reason, it is important to begin practicing neediness with people we trust and whom we believe will not violate vulnerability.

- *Spend time with children.* Psychiatrist Robert Coles, whose studies of children have opened up new avenues of understanding what it means to be human, has made this observation: "We are all children, and thank God we are. The problem is we don't know it well enough. This is one of the things Jesus taught us—to struggle toward childhood and never forget it or outlive it. And to retain in ourselves whatever shred of innocence and trust and willingness to engage ourselves with the world in the yearning and unashamedly vulnerable way that children possess."7 Learning from children the art of being vulnerable is necessary in order to discover our humanity as men.

It is difficult to live with vulnerability alone. When we become aware that being human means being susceptible to being wounded, we will long for the presence of others to sustain us in that awareness. The reluctance of men to acknowledge dependence makes it difficult to admit the need to be sustained by friends or communities of faith.

PRAYING AT NIGHT

Hebrew scholars tell us that Jacob was the first human being to pray at night.8 Before Jacob, encounters with God occurred in daylight and in the fullness of selfhood. By contrast, darkness and sleep seem to be the basic conditions for God's revelation to Jacob. When he was most vulnerable and not working at manipulating his destiny, God appeared to Jacob. Jacob experienced the presence of God the first time when he was on the way to Haran and exile with his uncle Laban. What Jacob hears is the same promise given to Abraham and Isaac. "All the families of the earth shall be blessed in you and in your offspring" (Gen. 28:14b). The heart of God's promise to Jacob is something quite dramatic and new. "Know that I am with you and will keep you wherever you go" (Gen. 28:15). For someone running in fear from an angry brother and *toward* an unknown future, that promise was enough to stop his fleeing. It is a good word as well for modern men who are running from the soul.

Jacob is not the only man ever to struggle with unseen forces in the night and discover in the process that he had been wrestling with God all along. Experiencing the light of God in the dark of night is like finding water in the wilderness, flowers in the desert, and resurrection in death. Perhaps the greatest challenge for men today who do not wake up from such encounters with an obvious limp is to risk even more vulnerability by sharing the experience with others. Unless, of course, the transformation is so profound that we walk, talk, and relate to others so differently (even without a limp) that it is obvious to others. Wrestling with God is not something men talk about easily because it is an admission of vulnerability. Taking that risk is what builds enduring bonds between men. In order to foster that risk, we need dependable friends and an environment safe enough to explore together the deep longings of the masculine soul. If we understand the church as "the community of the vulnerable ones," then it is such a safe place to talk about wrestling with God in the night.

Most of the time, when we long for a sign from God in the middle of confusing or dark days, we are looking for the assurance that God will not abandon us. The loneliness is not so intense nor the unpredictability of life so frightening when we can believe that God's promise to Jacob is for us as well. In spite of all Jacob's ambiguity, the promise to men and women today is that "the God of Jacob is our refuge" as well. Our ambiguity does not limit God's dependable presence. Vulnerability will not be eliminated. Nor is the future guaranteed. But God knows how much we need protection at every point of our lives. "Remember, I am with you" is the promise from God that conquers the fear of being wounded and thereby helps men to move toward fuller humanity.

DETERMINATION, AGGRESSION, AND VIOLENCE

Esau, as the biblical story tells it, was a man's man. "When the boys grew up, Esau was a skillful hunter, a man of the field, while Jacob was a quiet man, living in tents. Isaac loved Esau, because he was fond of game; but Rebekah loved Jacob" (Gen. 25:27–28). Esau lived by his strength; Jacob succeeded by cunning and wit. Although it would appear that Jacob was never physically aggressive, he was nonetheless very determined. Jacob's determination was supported by his mother, Rebekah, who encouraged him with the scheme to gain a blessing from his father, Isaac, by deceit. The way the story in Genesis enfolds, it would appear that Jacob's determination had the blessing of God.

Determination and deception got Jacob the blessing that belonged to his older twin, Esau. Jacob's determination made it possible for him to amass greater wealth and power than his cousins, the sons of Laban, for whom he worked. Again, when Jacob was in trouble, he fled rather than fight. "And Jacob deceived Laban the Aramean, in that he did not tell him that he intended to flee. So he fled with all that he had" (Gen. 31:20–21). Later, after wrestling with a stranger through the night, Jacob was terrified to hear that Esau was coming to meet him with four hundred men. "Jacob was greatly frightened; in his anxiety, he divided the people with him, and the flocks and herds and camels, into two companies, thinking, 'If Esau comes to the one company and destroys it, then the company that is left will escape'" (Gen. 32:8). It was a clever strategy meant to protect himself but in the process Jacob put others at risk. After the gracious encounter with Esau, Jacob refused Esau's invitation to travel together and settle near one another but rather took his own way. Mistrust and avoiding conflict were still a way of life for Jacob.

The story of Jacob is more about determination than violence. Determination is a virtue often ascribed to men who persevere against great odds to conquer the land, defeat enemies, gain wealth, or discover a cure for cancer. Being determined becomes a moral fault, however, when manipulation or deception are used to win and when people are violated even though no physical harm occurs. Assertion is another morally neutral dimension of human interaction used when a person seeks a desired goal by standing firm and negotiating vigorously. Assertion becomes aggression if the behavior brings psychological or physical injury to people or property. Aggression is a form of behavior that disregards the rights, thoughts, and feelings of others in order to achieve a desired goal. The focus of this chapter is on the connection between determination, aggression, and violence that has made it too easy for men over the centuries to justify violence as an unavoidable consequence of being determined.

Jacob was a determined man whom God used to continue the story of Israel as a people. Jacob was also a trickster who very cleverly manipulated situations to get what he wanted. Though Jacob's aggression did not physically harm others, he violated people through deception. That is one reason why it is easy to see the struggles of men today mirrored in Jacob's story. Aggressive behavior in men has been and continues to be problematic when it eventuates in violence toward others. Sometimes the aggressive action intends harm to others or damage to property. More often, however, people are hurt because they are in the way of aggressive action. Like a stray bullet that accidentally kills a child sitting on a porch, aggressive behavior claims innocent victims who simply happen to be in the wrong place at the wrong time. Determination in men too easily becomes aggression if achieving a goal is so important that the rights and well-being of people and property are incidental.

FIRE WITHOUT VIOLENCE

Determination has been a valued trait in men. It is a quality that drives men to succeed and seek to lead. Sometimes the same quality is referred to as persistence or stubbornness. *Sisu* is a Finnish word from my origins that conveys this spirit of perseverance. The quality to which *sisu* refers is best described as the "ability to penetrate a stone." Such determined behavior has been a highly valued male characteristic. We praise leaders who use determination to get what they want if it is what we want. We look for men to run corporations who are capable of overcoming resistance to achieve a goal. When men are rightly criticized for violent behavior, we often forget that violence is an easy extension of determination, which is promoted as a masculine virtue.

> It's a well-known fact that a male with even a moderate testosterone level would rather drill a hole in his hand (which he probably will) than admit, especially to his spouse, that he cannot do something himself. Put an ordinary husband on the Space Shuttle, and within minutes he'll be telling his spouse that . . . he'll repair the retro thruster modules, because if you call in NASA they'll just charge you an arm and a leg. I personally have destroyed numerous perfectly good rooms by undertaking frenzied testosterone-induced efforts to fix them up despite the fact that I have the manual dexterity of an oyster. Hundreds of years from now, archaeologists will look at my home-improvement projects and say: "This civilization was apparently wiped out by a terrible natural disaster involving spackle."
>
> Dave Barry, *Dave Barry's Complete Guide to Guys*

Aggressiveness in men has led to heroic deeds in defense of nation and family. It has also been occasion for unspeakable crimes of violence against other human beings. Male aggressiveness is frequently linked to the presence of testosterone in men. This reference to testosterone is meant to demonstrate that aggression is part of men's nature. When sufficient quantities of testosterone circulate in the blood, men grow beards, have erections, develop hard muscles and strong bones, and grow healthy and cancerous prostate tissue. It is also said that testosterone is the source of aggressiveness or rambunctious competitiveness that is both the blessing and the occasional curse of manliness. Too much testosterone, it is argued, prompts men to start wars or drive sport-utility vehicles and dominate whenever they can. The questions we face are these: How much male violence is socially constructed, learned, and therefore changeable by our choosing and how much is instinctive, innate, permanent, and therefore not easily changed? In a society that has programmed men to be violent, is it possible for men to be redeemed from violence without giving up their manhood?

Although it cannot be denied that men are affected by the presence of testosterone in their bodies, violent aggression or even rambunctious competitiveness can be regulated or controlled. The human creature is more than biology. Men and women alike are moral agents who decide whether or how to act on impulses. They are ethical actors who can choose to modify aggressive behavior in order to honor the rights of others. Even if we acknowledge the power of cascading testosterone in a man's life, he is still a moral agent who is free to decide how to use that power to act.

The problem with freedom is that it can be and is regularly abused. It is an even greater problem, however, for the future of humankind to assume that behavior can be reduced to biological causation. The character of a man is as important as his biology. Men don't need to fight a war, join a cigar club, or jump off a cliff with a bungee cord tied to our ankles to be manly. Joining a cigar club is easier than telling the CEO of your company or the guys at lunch break that you are teaching Sunday school. It takes just as much testosterone and courage to make friends with a needy kid or volunteer to cook at a homeless shelter as it does to destroy an enemy.

What is the Christian alternative to unchecked aggressiveness? How can men maintain "fire in the belly" without being violent? The biblical image of "saltiness" suggests a way to respect determination and passion in a peaceable fashion. Chapter 9 of Mark concludes with this verse: "Salt is good; but if salt has lost its saltiness, how can you season it? Have salt in yourselves, and be at peace with one another" (Mark 9:50). The image of salty peacefulness is parallel to tender aggression. The implication is that we can have salt in ourselves and still be at peace with one another. Salt is an aggressive spice. It penetrates food and brings out flavors without damaging other spices—unless, of course, there is too much salt. Young men cannot avoid saltiness or aggression. The task is to make sure there is not too much. As we age, too much salt can lead to health problems and so saltiness is replaced by other, more peaceable spices. The aim of faithfulness is not blandness but living peacefully with enough salt to keep passion alive and assertiveness focused.

Salty peacefulness introduces another paradox for our exploration of faithful Christian living. Christian communities of faith have been described as "salt factories," producing savor and zest for living without unchecked aggression or violence. The aim is to tame testosterone without eliminating appropriate male aggression. Nothing can be more important for our time. Men may learn how to grieve, promote friendship, or acknowledge vulnerability, but all those gains are canceled if male violence continues. Men need to choose to live constructively with testosterone until it declines. The recovery of determination and courage as male virtues and the practice of gentleness and compassion without undermining the values of aggression are strategies that require the best of men's energy. Christian manhood might then be described as tender aggression, salty peaceableness, or passion without violence.

REASONS FOR MEN'S VIOLENCE

There are other sources besides testosterone for violence among men. Recent brain research suggests that threatening environments may set off a chemical response in the brain of genetically susceptible people that may become the biochemical foundation for a lifetime of violent behavior. Some boys and men must grow up and live in contexts of poverty and racism that promote violence by producing cynicism and despair. School bullies will continue to taunt vulnerable classmates. Economic volatility and job instability generate frustration and hopelessness that put men on the edge of rage. Sharing feelings and learning to cope with disappointment may make it easier to avoid violent aggression but they do not eliminate rage. We also need to work towards modifying situations that might provoke or elicit aggressive behavior in men before they become violent.

This is a difficult chapter to write and read. People who are committed to civility in public and private contexts would like to exclude themselves from a picture of male anger and violent aggression. They abhor the increase of violence that has made the streets no longer safe for women and children and men as well. Our homes are no longer a place of safety for the vulnerable ones in our midst. Those who are appalled by the amount of violence in sports, films, and the news are reminded that ratings determine what sells. Movies and television rely too often on berserk violence as the ultimate image of potency. There is widespread concern that we have made violence a way of life. Violence seems to come to us naturally: the bully on the block, the soldier at war, the football hero, or the abusive husband all point to the commonness of violence.

Women and men alike participate in perpetuating a violent society. However, because the shooters in rampage killings are almost always boys or men, we cannot dispel the suspicion that the crimes of rage reveal something significant about the struggles of American men. "The women's movement," Dorothee Soelle has observed, "has repeatedly uncovered the connections between male dominance and war, between maleness and self-identification with the warrior, between lust and violence."[1] Men become violent when they are wounded, shamed, rejected, afraid, disappointed, powerless, humiliated, or filled with hate. It is as if violence is one response that fits all male pain.

Revenge

Revenge or "getting even" is one common source of violence. In a disturbing novel by John Burnham Schwartz entitled *Reservation Road*, a son is killed by a hit-and-run driver. The father of the boy who was killed is a professor. He says: "In the realm of fantasy I was a hard wronged man with a mission. This was a world of bright colors and clarity, quite the opposite of how things stood in real life. Never mind. This would be my story now. So nights I sat in my study and closed my eyes and killed the daylights out of a man I couldn't have identified had I passed him in the street. A nameless, faceless man." And then these painful words about revenge: "I want to be clear about this, now. Without hope, the need to punish is the one true religion. Blame must be fixed on some soul other than one's own. Justice must be done. Or else there is only the desert of grief and one's own footsteps upon it—restless, unceasing, as alone as the most distant planet in the universe."[2] These emotions are repeated in legal courtrooms where the survivors of a violent death insist that their grief will never be resolved unless one death is punished by another.

Retribution creates new victims and new demands for revenge. I have written elsewhere that "if justice is primarily understood as retribution, as it often is, the cycle of violence continues, and nothing changes."[3] The problem with revenge is that it is predicated on the assumption that healing the hurt comes by repeating the experience rather than cultivating empathy. Supplying the oppressor with an equally devastating experience of pain will not make it go away or change the story of suffering. In this sense, anger is wasted on revenge. The only way to stop the endless cycle of violence based on revenge is to enter the experience of the offender with imagination and empathy. "That kind of imagining another's story enables us to discover reconciliation beyond amnesia, beyond bargaining, and beyond revenge."[4] It is also empathy that enhances the possibility of forgiveness.

Frustration That Gets Out of Hand

When my daughter Joy taught in a Brooklyn high school, she had a student who needed to take an independent reading course in order to graduate. As an eighteen-year-old high school student, he already had a lucrative drug business, but he wanted to graduate to please his grandmother. His assignment was to read and write a report on the Pulitzer Prize-winning book on the Civil War entitled *Battle Cry of Freedom* by James McPherson. Joy loaned him my autographed copy of the book. Three weeks later, when the report on the book was due, the student called to say the assignment had been too much so he took the book down to the basement and shot it. That is both an outrageous and a deeply troubling story about the extent to which, at least in some corners of our society, violence is a socially acceptable way of solving problems or dealing with intolerable frustration.

What makes this pattern so deeply troubling is that there is less and less tolerance of frustration in this society as the pace of our lives increases. We are impatient with waiting, annoyed by inconvenience, outraged by incompetence, and pushed to violence by people who cut in ahead of us on the highway. We call it "road rage" and sometimes it leads to violence. It has often been said that there is little motivation for men to modify their violent behavior as long as society continues to promote violence in a variety of ways. Learning to live with frustration becomes another life strategy that takes courage and determination to achieve.

A Way of Gaining Control

The threat of violence is an effective means of maintaining control. The fear of violence has been used effectively by tyrants of all times and places to insure obedience and compliance. As long as men continue to expect to control their wives and children, even a little challenge to that dominance will sometimes elicit violence. Many children grow up in terror of their father's temper or his physical discipline. It may take only one violent outburst to establish fear that it could happen again unless people are compliant. The threat of violence establishes fathers or men in the power position. If children disobey or wives are not sufficiently compliant, men who are physically abusive will often say, "She (or he) had it coming." The need to control comes out of feelings of inadequacy and fear that must be covered over. If it is possible to control the other person, then men do not feel so inadequate or fearful. If violence helps men control their situation, then they do not have to think about inadequacy or fear in their lives.

Acts of violence toward partners in a relationship and children in families will continue until men and the larger society address the issue of dominance. James Dugo, a therapist who has worked with several hundred abusive men, is quite clear that "there's no way the rape's going to stop, or beating wives is going to stop, or beating kids is going to stop" until we change the social presumption of male control.5 Dugo believes that the inability to control anger before it turns violent is related to the inability to be vulnerable, express emotions other than anger, and learn to grieve. Men are violent because they can get by with it and because other constructive forms of passion are undeveloped. Two things seem clear: violence by men will continue until it is unacceptable in society and society forces a change; and men can avoid the impulse toward violence by learning to practice vulnerability.

James Poling is a pastoral theologian who has challenged churches to recognize their role in the perpetuation of violence against women and children. "How can violent men," Poling asks, "many of whom are Christians, engage in violence against women and children and not seek help from pastors and other caregivers? Because the churches have not identified male violence as a pressing ethical and religious issue [and] . . . because the church's patriarchal theology gives priority to the rights of men over women and children."6 In order for the churches to address the evil of male violence, the lingering support of male dominance in Christian theology must be challenged and changed.

The violent men I have worked with seem to learn their violence from two sources: (a) their own experiences of observing or experiencing violence during childhood; and (b) the power, privilege, and encouragement they get from race, gender, and class ideologies about dominance as a way of being. That is, race, gender, and class ensure that everyone will have some object to exploit in exchange for the abuse they endure from others. Even an abused child will be able to kick the dog, chase the cat, or mutilate the doll. . . . Men who engage in incest or abuse within the family seem to be an accurate reflection of the larger social forces. Perpetrators of family violence act with greater impunity whenever their chosen victims are less valued in the larger society, and when protection for children is less likely to be effective.

James Poling, *The Spirituality of Men*

Shaming

In street language, it is referred to as "dissing." In academic reflections on Roman life, it is referred to as "the honor code." The meaning is the same. It is a rigid patriarchal system reinforced by a culture of honor and shame. One mark of manliness is that we defend our honor and the honor of those we protect. Honor is gained by winning while dishonor or shame comes through losing. The authors of *From Culture Wars to Common Ground*, a book about the family debate in this society, note that protecting male honor is a central virtue. "For a man to avoid shame and for a woman to keep her shame, men had to protect, control, guide, and circumscribe the lives of their women so that their private space would not be dishonored. Such an ethic celebrated the virtues of active dominance for males and passive conformity for females."[7] This ancient honor code continues today when men are violent to protect family honor or when protecting male honor is used to justify violence toward a family member. In either instance, male dominance is presumed.

Rage

The *New York Times'* report of the tapes prepared by the young men referred to as the "Columbine killers" included several quotations from the tapes. "If you could see all the anger I've stored over the past four years," Mr. Klebod says, looking at the camera. "More rage, more rage," Mr. Harris says, "I'm building it up." Their action is described as payback against their enemies. "Isn't it fun," Mr. Harris says, "to get the respect that we're going to deserve?"[8] The origins of this rage include shame and humiliation. Rage that ends in violence is also the result of feeling powerless because of the loss of privilege, entitlement, or control. When a young man says, as a mark of being manly, that he is not afraid to kill and not afraid to die, he is speaking the language of young men who have gone to war over centuries of human history. If there is no war to fight, then such courage and determination are wasted on street battles or senseless violence.

The Warrior Metaphor

Being a warrior is one image that has embodied aggression in manhood for centuries. To be a warrior is to be the protector of hearth and home. It is also about conquest and control. In the past, men achieved warrior status through heroics on the battleground. Today, heroic warriors are made on the football field or through negotiating a corporate takeover. Whether the battleground is established in times of war, in the corporate boardroom, at a meeting of the zoning board, or on a basketball court, the dynamics of being a warrior are much the same.

It includes aggressiveness, clarity of thinking and acting, the willingness to risk in the face of apparent danger, and a loyalty to an ideal, the nation, winning, or a cause that relativizes all personal relationships.[9]

When being a warrior is the dominant metaphor for being a man, there is also the danger that women are to be protected, conquered, possessed, and, if necessary, humiliated or sexually violated. Consider the following stories from the sports section of the *Seattle Post-Intelligencer* on Inauguration Day, Saturday, January 20, 2001.

- A running back for the Cincinnati Bengals paid $750 to a woman's shelter and was required to undergo eighteen months of certified abuse treatment for fourth-degree assault against his wife.

- Former National Football League player Rae Carruth was acquitted of first-degree murder but convicted of conspiracy to commit murder and two other charges in the shooting death of his pregnant girl-friend in order to avoid paying child support.

- Jason Kidd, All-Star point guard for the Phoenix Suns, was charged with misdemeanor assault for hitting his wife in an argument over feeding their two-year-old son.

- The Seattle Sonics played a basketball game without their star guard Gary Payton, who was suspended one game for a public verbal tirade toward the coach and his teammates. The headline the next day in the same sports section read, "Can Payton Combine Fire and Nice?" It was, the sportswriter admitted, a daunting challenge. The team hopes that Payton can maintain his warrior-like aggressive mentality and play without crossing the line. Being nice may be asking too much. After Payton's return won a game for the Sonics, it was reported that "great ability and the ability to grate" go hand in hand.

These headlines not only illustrate how much athletic heroes in the United States have gone beyond controlled violence in the game to violent behavior in life. They point to larger and more disturbing questions for modern men seeking to be faithful to God: can men be passionate and aggressive without being violent? I hope by now the answer is both clear and convincing: although aggression is unavoidable and violence always possible, Christian men can live in ways that honor determination without violence.

BACK TO JACOB: DETERMINATION AND RECONCILIATION

We are looking at the story of Jacob's wrestling with a stranger by the river Jabbok from a number of angles. In this discussion of determination and violence, Jacob's anticipated and feared meeting with Esau puts before us the ongoing need for reconciliation with those we have violated or who have offended us. There is a strong impulse to suppress the memory of violence or wrongdoing in the false hope that we can put the violent history behind us and move more steadily toward reconciliation. We can imagine that Jacob hoped for such a reunion. This kind of reconciliation is often advocated by perpetrators of violence who realize the consequences of their actions and seek to erase them from memory. Robert Schreiter has reminded us that the move to a hasty peace is the opposite of reconciliation because "the victim is forgotten and the causes of suffering are never uncovered or confronted."[10] While we could not say that Jacob's desire for peace was hasty after all of his years in exile, there is no indication from the narrative that Jacob acknowledged his offense or the hurt he caused to Esau. One can only assume that the abundance of gifts was intended to cover over the memory.

Each of us has our Jabbok—a moment when we must face ourselves and God for truth and then for healing. In order to determine how your own story mirrors the story of Jacob wrestling with a messenger from God at Jabbok, you might bring to mind a close relationship in your life in need of reconciliation.

- It may have happened just last night when a child came home late from a date and you exploded with more rage than she deserved. The intensity of your rage came from a conflict with your work supervisor.

- You may have learned just Thursday about someone you had unintentionally offended at a church meeting by not asking his or her opinion about something.

- The conflict may be between you and your spouse. The last argument was messy. It is an open sore at the moment and neither of you is willing to take the first step to say, "I'm sorry."

- You may have been abused by your father as a child and it is only in the last year that you have remembered that painful time. When you confronted your father, he denied everything and accused you of being brainwashed by your feminist friends. And now, to make things more difficult, your father has cancer and has only a short time to live.

- It may be that you are harboring old resentments toward parents or siblings from long ago when an estate was divided and you did not get your fair share. What you had long suspected turned out to be true: your sister was grandmother's favorite.

- It may even be that your story is in Jacob's shadow. Long ago you tricked your brother out of something that was rightfully his and you have been estranged ever since.

PEACEMAKERS INSTEAD OF WARRIORS

The warrior will remain a metaphor for being a man. It is, however, a limited metaphor if men want to change the patterns of violence that we use to dominate others and that in turn rule our lives. The authors of *From Culture Wars to Common Ground* suggest that the "new male ethic, like the new male armor, is an ethic of peace."[11] Being a peacemaker shifts determined behavior away from conquest and control toward harmony and cooperation. It is a vision of being a man that longs for an end to domination of any kind. To be a peacemaker is to be willing to make compromises and sacrifices for the sake of loyalty to a larger vision. Being a peacemaker means believing that people can be together, think together, work together, play together, even intensely and aggressively, in ways that are cooperative and collegial. Being a peacemaker takes determination.

> The male paradigm of confrontation, in which an enemy could be identified, contested, and defeated, was endlessly transferable. It proved useful as well to activists in the civil-rights movement and the antiwar movement, the gay-rights movement and the environmental movement. . . . Yet it could launch no "men's movement." Herein lies the bedeviling paradox, and the source of male inaction: the model women have used to revolt is the exact one men not only can't use but are trapped in. . . . [Men today are] faced with a historic opportunity: to learn to wage a battle against no enemy, to own a frontier of human liberty, to act in the service of a brotherhood that includes us all.
>
> Susan Faludi, *Stiffed: The Betrayal of the American Man*

In the mid-80s, the United Presbyterian Church in the United States of America undertook a special four-year emphasis on the theme "Peacemaking: The Believers' Calling."[12] It included a comprehensive challenge to practice the vocation of peacemaking in a variety of places in the world and in the church, but there was no mention of the family. The document is a bold challenge to work for justice in the global context and to address issues related to national policy from the perspective of peacemaking. I mention this document not to criticize the Presbyterian Church but to note how easy it is to segregate the public and the private spheres. It is possible for a man to work at peacemaking in the public sphere, be abusive or aggressive in the home, and not understand the contradiction in that behavior. The churches have been silent on male violence to women and children for much too long. The present focus of Men's Ministries on abuse is a timely effort to rectify the silence.

To be a peacemaker is to know the peace of Christ deep enough to live in a way that creates communities that are peaceable. The possibility of making and keeping peace requires the skill of negotiation and the willingness to acknowledge that two ideas may both be good or two conclusions may both be true. In order for that to be possible for men, we will need to learn a little humility about ourselves and a lot of respect for the validity of the other. The apostle Paul addressed the honor code and the ethos of dominance and privilege for men by imploring them to live "with all humility and gentleness, with patience, bearing with one another in love, making every effort to maintain the unity of the Spirit in the bond of peace" (Eph. 4:2–3). That is a vision that invites all men to live lives of "salty peacefulness" in Christ.

Chapter

4

EXPRESSING FEELINGS

When Isaac and Esau discovered they had been deceived by Jacob and Rebekah, their emotional response was immediate and intense. "Then Isaac trembled violently, and said, 'Who was it then that hunted game and brought it to me, and I ate it all before you came, and I have blessed him?—yes, and blessed he shall be!' When Esau heard his father's words, he cried out with an exceedingly great and bitter cry, and said to his father, 'Bless me, me also, father!' But [Isaac] said, 'Your brother came deceitfully, and he has taken away your blessing.' 'What then can I do for you, my son?' Esau said to his father, 'Have you only one blessing, father? Bless me, me also, father!' And Esau lifted up his voice and wept" (Gen. 27:33–38). Their loss was immense and their pain was not hidden.

Frederick Buechner's fictitious account of Jacob's life portrays an attitude toward expressing feelings that has been more common among men. In a private conversation, Isaac (whose name means "laughter") is telling Jacob the story about how his own father, Abraham, almost sacrificed Isaac to please the gods. "It was the worst moment of my life up till then," Jacob observes. "I was so ashamed of Laughter's weeping that I thought I was going to be sick. I wanted to run out of the tent so that I would not have to see his tears. . . . It was slovenly, shameful weeping. Dribble ran out of Laughter's nose. . . . He blubbered like a woman. His whole thick frame shook. I squatted by the smoking dung staring at him."[1] From biblical times until now, two things are certain. Men have emotions, and men are not always comfortable expressing what they feel or even being in the presence of intense emotions they cannot change.

Men, it is said, do not express their feelings easily. As a result, the operative myth about men has been that they are unemotional. The truth is that men have emotions but struggle to express them. In the biblical account, Jacob's pain was not hidden. When Buechner tells the story, Jacob is embarrassed as a young man because his father Isaac "blubbered like a woman." Jacob's reaction follows the traditional gender stereotypes about expressing feelings. Women do, men don't. However, both women and men believe that inside the controlled exterior of men is a sea of emotions that simply have no outlet. Not expressing emotions has proven to be socially beneficial. Men respect and fear other men whose feelings are hidden and well-defended. Women are often drawn to men whose feelings lie dormant beneath a facade of mastery and control but are disappointed if men cannot express what they feel. When men are pressed to express what they feel, they are likely to be silent and the cycle continues. Male reluctance to express feelings is a long-standing pattern with serious consequences not only for men but also for women and the relationships between women and men.

SHE SAYS LOTS, HE SAYS VERY LITTLE

Studies in communication between husbands and wives have identified ways in which the inability to express feelings is detrimental to a healthy marriage. Deborah Tannen has described a typical conversation at the end of a day.

The same man who dominates the board meeting comes home at the end of the day to a woman who will tell him everything that happened to her during the day—if she was home, what the children did and said, where she went and whom she met, who called to tell what news. If she was at work, she will tell him about the people at work, what this or that colleague said, what happened at the meeting, what she said and how it was received. Then she turns to him and asks, "How was your day?"

And he replies: "Okay."

Hurt, she presses, "Didn't anything happen at work?" "Nope," he answers, honestly. "It was just a day like any other." Or he might say, "I had a rotten day; I just want to relax." "What happened?" she encourages, eager to hear his woes. "Oh, nothing special. It was just a rough day, that's all. The usual."[2]

A woman may conclude from such a conversation that (1) something is wrong with her because he won't talk, (2) they aren't as close as they should be, (3) there is lack of real communication, or (4) that her husband is deficient because he is not in touch with his feelings and doesn't share. She feels marginalized because he doesn't tell her anything that is going on in his life. Her husband, on the other hand, has been working in a stress-filled environment and the challenge from his wife to talk about feelings is even more stress than he experienced all day. When both wives and husbands have jobs outside the home, they may talk more about what happened even though men will still struggle with the expression of vulnerable emotions.

One of the secrets to a happy marriage, according to Laura Doyle's book *The Surrendered Wife*, is that a wife should express herself in terms of what she feels rather than what she thinks, but she should never ask her husband about his feelings. The assumption is not so much that men have no feelings but rather that they are not able to express their feelings easily. Furthermore, Doyle argues, women who are nagging and faultfinding are likely to turn the man they love into a helpless lump of resentment and passive aggression. Even after they have been encouraged to express what they feel, men are silent. The end result of persistent criticizing of men for not expressing emotions is usually more silence.[3]

I do not agree with Doyle's recipe for marriage. Her description of men reinforces the stereotype that we are struggling to overcome. If the only way to have a happy marriage is that women accommodate the deficiencies of men, then we will all be diminished. Women will maintain emotional superiority and men will not be challenged to change. Furthermore, being the one accommodated puts men in the position of weakness rather than strength. Craig's marriage makes this point. He is quite clear to his friends that he married not only for love but also because he needed someone to tell him what he was feeling. After fifteen years of marriage, the asymmetrical pattern remains. Craig's work is a highly public executive position. Nonetheless, he regularly confers with Roberta for input about what he is feeling. Roberta is willing to oblige this expectation because it is a way for her to stay close to Craig.

Peter told a similar story. He grew up in a Roman Catholic family in which the primary authority belonged to his mother and the nuns at St.

Jude Parish. "My father was a dependent and depressed person who relied on my mother and *his* mother to guide his life for him. This was my view of 'maleness' as a child and I rejected it in favor of the strength which to me seemed to be a female trait. Ironically, my family rewarded the expression of feelings. Whoever was the saddest, angriest, most depressed determined what happened. My father actually modeled this well. He was needy and weak and his emotions ruled our house. He got his way by whining or pouting. My maternal grandfather was a sentimental man who would cry openly over a sad poem, the death of a pet, or an insult from a loved one. At thirty, I am comfortable as a gay man but I still do not have a good sense of maleness."

Of course, these stories do not reveal the whole truth. Not all men are silent, unable to express what they feel, or manipulative out of neediness. Many men have learned to tell about the activities of a day and be attentive as women tell about theirs. Men are discovering an inner world of deeply held emotions that has power to shape our relationships with others and improve our cardiovascular system. More and more men are comfortable expressing affectionate, vulnerable feelings to family and trusted friends. From a variety of perspectives, including a more wholistic view of the human person, men are learning the benefits of sharing feelings and speaking from the heart.

THE UNTUTORED HEART

The inability to express feelings is not a moral fault for men. It is the result of *an untutored heart*. The challenges of survival or the risks of untamed land and terrifying seas were enough to occupy the attention of men for many centuries. Simon Carr writes about his experience as a father raising his two sons. The youngest son was five when his mother died after a four-year battle with cancer. Alexander compartmentalized his emotions for weeks in a way that is characteristically male. "Dealing with such emotions was new and not easy for someone with an untutored heart. I had never taken a proper interest in how these things work, and had been content to delegate much to Susie [deceased wife], who had real talent for how people felt."[4] It was his sons, Simon Carr admits, who tutored his heart and taught him to treasure his emotional economy.

Old masculine myths continue to whisper in our modern ears, despite these positive changes. In his book *Counseling Men*, Philip Culbertson describes the male dilemma with emotions: "Patriarchal masculinity denigrates and trivializes the world of inner experience, feeling, and intuition."[5] This quotation helps men understand why they have overlooked their inner world and are reluctant to express feelings. We disregard what is trivial. More than that, we look with disdain on men who acknowledge vulnerability or weakness. Residues of patriarchy today continue to connect between expressing emotions and being vulnerable. For men to acknowledge feelings like sadness, despair, or anxiety even to themselves depends on a willingness to be vulnerable.

> Many of the boys with whom I grew up have been expert "homoclites." They can't think and feel at the same time. They try not to think about how they feel and they try to stop those around them from stimulating any emotion. They are disoriented by issues that can't be settled by choosing True or False; they really hate essay questions because they don't tolerate doubt. They want life to be like baseball, played dispassionately with incontestable rules, lots of statistics, referees at every corner to make sure that everyone does the right thing, and the game played out until there is a clear winner.
>
> Frank Pittman, *Man Enough: Fathers, Sons, and the Search for Masculinity*

One Presbyterian man I spoke with while writing this book was very clear about his expectations. "Could you please address issues of insulation from feelings," he said, "which seems to be a major source of isolation in men and separation from children, wives, and the church?" While the entire book seeks to address that question, the aim of this chapter in particular is to encourage men to discover our inner world, decrease the need to express anger and rage in inappropriate ways, and increase our ability to speak directly about feelings of loneliness, sadness, fear, hurt, affection, and gratitude. The following story from a close friend named George describes one man's struggle with expressing feelings.

My history with tears begins in childhood. My childhood tears are a part of myself that I have not understood very well. I was a small, thin, notably weak kid, easily threatened, frightened, or intimidated. My father called me a smart aleck, however, because I used my wit and my mouth in aggressive defense to compensate for my internal pain. The first specific time of tears I recall was when I was being examined for the rank of Second Class Scout. I was a good scout. I had studied the

Handbook and I knew my stuff cold. I knew how to tie a square knot and build a simple latrine on a granite cliff. As the examination went on, my lips began to quiver, my voice got shaky, and I knew I was on the verge of tears. I had no idea what I was crying about or how to stop the crying. The committee thought it might be the cigar smoke. Nonetheless I finished the exam and was promoted to Second Class Scout. I never told anyone about crying.

This experience made me apprehensive as I approached the Committee for promotion to First Class. No amount of will power was effective. The experience of crying repeated itself then and at the next two reviews as well. By the time I was interviewed for Eagle Scout, Scouting's highest rank, I was prepared for the tears. Sure enough, they came again. This time I was more adept at helping the committee ignore it and not get worried about my crying. Not long before that, I was the youth leader for our Sunday school program and the tears came again. There I stood, trying to read my little meditation and trying to pretend I wasn't crying. It was puzzling and embarrassing. After the Eagle Scout Committee I stopped crying until my sister's wedding, when Dad's sobs choked me up.

It was the biggest gift my Dad had ever given me. My story of tears is about the power and the repression of feelings, and the denial of what they reveal. It is also a story about small steps I have taken in overcoming that repression in order to trust the inspiration of my feelings. It is a story about learning to be a man in a society where men don't cry.

George's wrestling with the angel of tears introduces many themes that will reoccur in other chapters. Everything is connected to everything else, even in the world of feelings. So, for example, admitting vulnerability precedes men's willingness to touch their inner world. George did not know the meaning of the tears before he felt them. Being able to grieve the losses of our lives flows from the practice of expressing emotions when they occur in everyday situations like becoming an Eagle Scout. The inability of men to control the expression of anger is explored in the chapter on aggression and violence, but I mention it here as well because it is the emotion men express most readily.

THE EMOTION MEN WILL EXPRESS: ANGER

While there are many variations among men in showing feelings, it is nonetheless generally true that men express some emotions more readily than others. *Aggression and anger are widely accepted in this society as necessary, even inevitable, characteristics of being a man.* Men learn very young to equate anger with aggression. James and Evelyn Whitehead propose that American fathers intentionally make their sons angry and then channel that feeling into aggressive behavior. Fathers berate sons in public, call them belittling names, set impossible achievement standards, and mock them when they fail. The anger that is generated, however, cannot be expressed toward the father. Instead, "boys learn to use their anger to compete, to contest, to win out over others, to best the opponent—all skills required to make it in a man's world."[6] For men more than for women, anger is readily expressed in public. When guys disagree, someone told me long ago, they work things out with their fists.

Boys learn two things from the experience with their fathers that dominate their lives as men. First, anger is unacceptable. So are the feelings of fear, hurt, and shame that accompany those early experiences of provoked and repressed anger. To keep anger in check, a man's inner world is hidden even from himself and unavailable to those nearby. "Second, the little boy learns to connect feeling vulnerable with acting aggressively. . . . Many men continue this pattern as adults, responding combatively in situations where they feel weak or vulnerable."[7] This analysis of how boys learn to relate to anger helps to explain why men frequently respond to vulnerability with anger and violent behavior.

Although there is evidence that some violent acts have decreased, the pervasive presence of rage among men in this society is still alarming. The vast majority of violent crimes (nine of every ten) are committed by men. Every day there are news reports of murder, mayhem, and other destructive behavior by men and boys. As I wrote this chapter, there was a news report of a man who killed three residents of a retirement home and then killed himself because he was denied admittance. Road rage is another troubling sign that anger has become a public health issue. Hate crimes are the result of chronic anger fueled by an attitude of superiority or condescension toward despised groups or individuals. Despite efforts to alter male attitudes toward women, girls and women around the globe are vulnerable to particular kinds of violence perpetrated by men such as domestic violence, rape, incest, and so-called honor crimes. It is much too common for men (and boys) who are frustrated or angry to hurt, punish, or even eliminate what provokes their anger. These instances illustrate that unmanaged male anger continues to hurt people, destabilize society, and diminish men.

Anger is a necessary human emotion even though it is complicated. It signals that there is a problem that needs to be addressed, identifies injustice or evil, and mobilizes our efforts to correct the ill. Anger strengthens our desire to protect from harm people we love or ideas we value. When we are angry, we are more likely to stand up for ourselves.

The more we learn to respect human difference, the more likely we will encounter conflict and even anger between people who do not agree. In order to prevent ordinary anger from escalating into hatred or violence, we need to relearn rules of civility. If we cannot find room for anger within ordinary, civil discourse, it will remain on the margins of ordinary communication and make the cultural heritage of violence the norm.

Feelings Men Have Difficulty Expressing

There are times in men's lives when we react emotionally to a situation but do not know what provoked such a strong reaction, nor are able to name the particular feelings. It would be enough for us to say that we reacted strongly to one thing or another in the situation. Identifying the content of that emotional reaction would require a willingness to explore the forbidden territory of one's inner world. When men are reluctant to be in silence, it is usually out of fear for what might be discovered in that unknown territory. The presumption is that the inner self is dominated by negative emotions. Nonetheless, I was quite certain I could identify the feelings men have difficulty expressing until I took a very unscientific survey and did not find any pattern.

The male struggle to express feelings varies with personality differences and family influence. For some men, affectionate feelings are easily expressed; other men are more comfortable with sadness, still others with joy. Shy men may also know fear; gregarious men may be familiar with loneliness. I grew up in a family in which pride was never acceptable. If anyone bragged a little too much about some success, my father would say something like, "Pride goes before the fall." On the other hand, worry and depression were the emotions guaranteed to evoke a sympathetic response from everyone in the family. My mother, I have often said, was a world-class worrier. Unfortunately, she taught me well. I can find rain clouds in a blue sky.

What I also learned from my unscientific poll of women and men is that there are patterns of thinking and perspectives on living that impede showing feelings. For example, as long as men remain primarily linear thinkers, they will insist that things are either A or B and resist ambiguity. Because emotions are by definition ambiguous, they need to be ignored in favor of definitive, linear thinking, praised by men as the rational and normative way to think. A woman therapist I know who has worked with men in counseling for many years suggested that men need to appear independent even when their behavior suggests otherwise. That means, she observed, that the words and the music do not always fit. If I am particularly loud at a party, my wife will know that I am anxious before I do. As long as she continues to know what I feel first, I remain an untutored heart, continue to resent her, and never learn how to identify what is stirring in my inner world.

Plainsong is a novel by Kent Haruf that exquisitely conveys the struggles men have to express what they feel. Part of the story centers around Raymond and Harold McPheron, bachelor brother farmers who decide to take in seventeen-year-old Victoria, who is pregnant and needs a home. She is with them for an awkward while and then, without telling the brothers, leaves with the unborn child's father. Eventually Victoria returns and the brothers take her back. In describing the scene of her return, Haruf captures the painful difficulty men have expressing their deep emotions.

> The old brothers stood regarding her without speaking, without moving. It was as though they didn't know her or didn't want to remember what they knew about her. She couldn't say what they were thinking. I hope you're both well, she said. I won't be bothering you anymore. She turned to go back to the car.
>
> She was halfway to the gate when Harold spoke. We couldn't have you leaving like that again, he said.
>
> She stopped. She turned around to face them. I know, she said. I wouldn't.
>
> We wouldn't want that again. Not ever. . . . That has to be understood.[8]

As night gathered around the horse barn, the two brothers and the pregnant girl went inside the old house and sat at the kitchen table. Victoria could see that things had fallen into disorder since she left. Harold McPheron made coffee.

> The old house was quiet, just the wind and the sound of the food beginning to heat on the stove.
>
> You had us worried, Raymond said. He was looking at her, sitting beside her at the table. We got worried about it. We didn't know where you was. We didn't know what we might of done to cause you to want to leave here like that.
>
> But you didn't do anything, the girl said. It wasn't you.
>
> Well. We didn't know what it was.
>
> It wasn't you at all, she said. Oh, I'm sorry. I'm so sorry. She began to cry then. The tears ran down her cheeks and she tried to wipe them away, but she couldn't keep up. She didn't make any sound at all while she was crying.
>
> The two old brothers watched her uncomfortably. Here now, Raymond said. It's all right. We won't have any of that now. We're glad if you come back.

I didn't mean to cause any trouble, she said.

Well no, he said. We know. That's all right. Don't you mind it now. It's all right now. He reached across the table and tapped the back of her hand. It was a clumsy act. He didn't know how to manage it. Don't you mind it, he said to her. If you come back here we're glad. Don't you mind it now anymore.[9]

In a way, the McPheron brothers are every man. They cared deeply for Victoria and they were glad to have her back but they could not say it. It was also difficult for them to be in the presence of her tears not knowing what to do. The dilemma is that Victoria must read between the lines and interpret the clumsy gestures to be assured that it is all right that she has come back. Men ask a great deal of others when they expect others to know our unexpressed emotions. And men, ironically, must trust others to get it right. It would be a lot simpler and clearer if men could express the deep tenderness they feel.

WHEN EMOTIONS ARE INTOLERABLE

Being strong and presenting a winning image also make it difficult for men to be honest about failure, disappointment, or even a minor mistake that could damage a public image of competence and control. While there is no particular virtue in public exposure of human failing, the need to promote a successful self-image has sometimes led to seriously damaging patterns of self-deception. When pretense is coupled with arrogance, men have paid a terrible price for always needing to be perceived as successful. Authenticity in human interaction is one way of describing a new way of being a man that combines honesty with strength.

The inability to acknowledge or admit to strong emotions within is one dilemma for men. Sometimes, however, we may know what we feel but cannot tolerate it. That is certainly the case in cultures where shame is the forbidden emotion. Saving face will lead men (and women) to self-destructive acts in order to avoid public shame or responsibility for having brought shame to a family. Fear is an emotion that often results in destructive acts. Boys are taught to be brave. It is bravery and courage that has led men to face death in war or risk their lives in dangerous adventure. In order to be brave, men have been expected to hide their fear. The inability to acknowledge fear creates an artificial confidence that has no ground when fear can no longer be avoided. Anger, we have already said, is usually a precursor to violence. But so is terror.

Mark O. Barton was the thirty-four-year-old day trader from Alabama who killed three people in a shooting spree precipitated by terror and hopelessness. "I wake up at night so afraid, so terrified that I couldn't be that afraid while awake. I have come to hate this life and this system of things."[10] To be a man has always been to receive and pass on a patrimony of skills and a place within a system. But many men suspect that all they have inherited are their fathers' fears—of being found wanting, incapable, not needed, without the tools to deal with those fears. Because it is very difficult to express fear directly, it often comes out as violence as it did for Mark Barton.

Learning to live with fear is one way to stem the tide of male violence in situations that provoke intolerable fear. If, however, men must continue to hide vulnerability, then violent or aggressive behavior will continue to harm others in order to mask terror. Acknowledging fear does not necessarily inhibit brave action; it simply humanizes the warrior.

Jack Galvin's life has been overflowing with good fortune. He would be the first to admit it. He is happily married to his high school sweetheart for thirty-nine years. They have three grown children who are also happily married and twelve grandchildren. His printing business is not what it used to be but they are financially secure and in good health. For all of that, when Jack was asked about emotions he had difficulty expressing, he very quickly named two: gratitude and joy. When we explored his response together, it became clear to Jack that his reluctance to express joy was part of his need to keep control in his life; and not showing the gratitude he felt avoided acknowledging dependence. Jack had worked very hard to achieve what he had. While Jack would say he was happy, it was sometimes difficult to tell. He missed a lot of childhood because he started working for his grandfather in the print shop at age twelve. Jack remembers his grandfather saying regularly, "You can't sit on the hill and feel the breeze on your face unless you own the hill." Although Jack was an active member of his church, he could not agree with the emphasis on gratitude in his pastor's sermons. For Jack, always having to say thank you meant that he was more dependent in his life than he was willing to admit.

One theme in this book is the recognition that some areas of human behavior underdeveloped in men are the result of the over-development of other practices that have been socially approved or even required. So, for example, along with being physically strong, men have been expected to control their feelings in order to remain calm in the midst of crisis and chaos or exercise rationality when a situation is in danger of getting out of hand. Maintaining control and stoic endurance have been ways to exercise responsibility in social situations. As a result, men have emotions but no easy way to access them or express them directly. For men to discover that expressing emotions is a necessary dimension of their full humanity, they will also need to learn to share responsibility and modify the expectation that there are other ways to be in charge without maintaining rational control. Jack would be more likely to express gratitude if he could understand that dependence is part of the human condition and not a sign of weakness.

BECOMING PASSIONATE MEN AS PART OF FAITH

Men are passionate creatures. Being passionate has been regarded as a sign of strength in men. It is also a gift for faith. A living faith is sustained by the gracious compassion of God and the human passion for justice. The passion for truth has led men to great adventures and terrible atrocities. That passion can be expressed in lovemaking, the care of children, and commitment to friendship. Other times, passions erupt into violence. The aim of this chapter has been to encourage the expression of emotions like sadness or compassion that have been less revered in men. Men will be free to show emotions when we learn to be comfortable with other aspects of being human like dependence, ambiguity, and vulnerability. At the same time, there are some concrete things we can do to enhance the practice of expressing feelings.

Befriend our feelings. If we are able to make friends with the feelings that disturb us, they will (1) teach us about what we value, (2) evoke passions that can be transformed into constructive energy and reliable virtues, and (3) become allies in modifying what harms or disturbs. In order to befriend our feelings, we need to have the courage to hold still long enough to recognize what we are feeling. Such patience, James and Evelyn Whitehead suggest, "is not a placid compliance, but a courageous attention to the turns and invitations of our life."[11] What we may discover is that some of our passions are dangerous because we may harm others or injure ourselves, but most of our passions promote life.

Name them accurately. Feelings resemble one another. It is sometimes difficult, for example, to tell when annoyance becomes irritation and irritation becomes anger. Hurt and anger are common bedfellows. Sadness, grief, depression, and despair share common characteristics even though they may feel very different on the inside. If we know the difference between vindication and vengeance, we can live with anger more easily. There is a greater chance of developing mastery over troubling emotions if we can name them accurately. We may begin simply by determining whether we feel glad, mad, sad, or bad.

Identify the origins of the feelings. Even when we are not able to say what we feel, it is useful to explore what provoked the emotional disturbance. That may include asking other questions like, "When did we first begin to have the feeling?" or "Can we associate the emotion with a particular situation or person?" I can speak to hundreds, but when I ask a question in a seminar or intellectual gathering, my palms sweat and my voice changes. A woman friend once observed that men are more passionate than women and more likely to allow their emotions to carry them away. If that is true, and I think it is, then it is very important for men to understand where they come from and what fuels their passions. We cannot claim, control, or reject what we do not understand.

Allow disciplined emotions to motivate action. The Whiteheads write, "Emotions stir us first as physiological arousals, then elicit an interpretation of their meaning, and then impel us to act. Emotions are feelings that move us: they generate *movement*."[12] In order that we might channel or discipline emotions into positive action, we need to acknowledge that they exist within us and then gain some mastery over the emotions. We have the emotions rather than the emotions have us. If we have emotions, we can learn how to put them to good use.

Recognize that feelings are not permanent unless we make them so. As an adolescent with ordinary feelings of lust, I regularly felt condemned by one saying of Jesus. "But I say to you that everyone who looks at a woman with lust has already committed adultery with her in his heart" (Matt. 5:28). I was overwhelmed with Swedish Lutheran guilt until I was liberated by the following line attributed to Martin Luther: "You can't stop the birds from flying over your head but you can prevent them from building a nest in your hair." Feelings come and go. They are, by definition, unplanned, unannounced, and spontaneous. Even negative emotions like anger and fear become a problem only when they take up permanent residence within us.

Faithfulness includes moving from passivity to participation. What we have been exploring together in this chapter is a movement from being victims of hidden emotions to responsible participation in the passionate life. The way of Jesus is embrace and not control. In the company of Jesus and other men who take the courage to walk the road, we learn how to live with strong emotions in a way that transforms them into creative and faithful passions.

You remember my friend George, the Eagle Scout. He wrote his "story of tears" not long after he left the Reformed Church to become a Quaker.

He met with four members of the Friends Meeting to gain clearness about whether the faith he had come to recognize within was consistent with their understanding of Quaker faithfulness. He spoke to them about some of the painful times of self-depreciation in his life and how his experience with the Calvinist doctrine of total depravity reinforced those negative emotions.

> As I spoke, I felt my lips quivering again and my voice getting shaky again and the tears rolling down my face for the first time since I became an Eagle Scout. In meeting with the Friends I felt like I could be myself in all of my uncertainty and pain, in all of my anger and my struggle to find a faith that was life-giving for me. I felt like I had found companions in the wilderness after years of being out there alone. My tears expressed the joy of that discovery.

I hope all men who read this book will find a church home that will (1) be a safe place to tutor the heart, (2) support the struggle to discover the best in themselves, (3) provide companions for encouragement, and (4) foster an environment in which they will feel free to let the tears roll.

PROMISING

The blessing given to a first-born is a gift and a burden. It is the assurance of an honored place in a human community. That is the gift. At the same time, being the "blest one" carries with it expectations of being responsible, being in charge, and making things happen. That is the burden. Over and over again, God reminded Jacob of the consequences of being blessed. "I am God Almighty: be fruitful and multiply; a nation and a company of nations shall come from you, and kings shall spring from you" (Gen. 35:11). God was responsible for Israel's success. Although Jacob suffered many losses, he prospered according to the promises of God. When he was with Laban, Jacob worked hard and his wealth grew. After his meeting with Esau, Jacob flourished in the land of Caanan. God kept promising.

Jacob was a gentle patriarch after his days of deception were over. When there was famine in the land of Caanan and the only way to survive was to buy grain from Egypt, Jacob's sons unknowingly encountered their brother Joseph, whom they had sold to slave traders. This time, Joseph was the deceptive one.

Without revealing his identity, Joseph tested his brothers by demanding that they bring their youngest brother (Benjamin) if they were to get any more grain. Jacob balked. He was too vulnerable to risk losing a beloved child of his old age. "'I am the one you have bereaved of children: Joseph is no more, and Simeon is no more, and now you would take Benjamin. All this has happened to me!'" (Gen. 42:36). Jacob would not allow Benjamin to go to Egypt until the people of Israel ran out of food again and the famine was severe. Jacob's commitment to provide for the well-being of his people was in conflict with his need to hold on to his youngest son and the child of Rachel. For men today, as for Jacob, making and keeping promises often includes choosing between two commitments of equal value.

Human beings are promise makers. We make promises in many contexts and for many reasons. As children, we promise to clean our room or keep a secret. We promise to be a buddy and then seal that promise with the vow "cross my heart and hope to die." When we marry, we promise to be a lifelong covenant partner. After we are married, we promise to pick up our socks, be on time for dinner, pick up the kids from school, order theatre tickets, and carry out the garbage. When we take an oath, we promise to tell the truth. It is a matter of law. When we promise our boss that we will finish the report on time or promise people who care about us that we will change our ways or take responsibility for our action, keeping that promise is a moral act rather than a legal matter. Most of the time, we intend to keep the promises we make and be where we promise to be, or do what we promise to do. Our promises are simple and complex, foolish and wise, individual and communal, formal and informal. Promises hold us together and keep us apart. As the philosopher Hannah Arndt once observed, promising is the sacrament of the will. It is what humans do.

WHAT DOES PROMISING MEAN?

Although promising is something humans do easily, keeping the promises we make is harder to do. Not keeping our commitments or breaking a promise is much too common. In fact, making and keeping commitments has been described as a problem in this society. According to one author, Barbara Dafoe Whitehead, the frequency of divorce in the United States has created what she calls a "low commitment culture." The change is away from "an ethic of obligation and toward an obligation to self."[1] Looking out for and being responsible for one's own needs and interests are regarded as the primary moral obligation of a low commitment culture.

For men, this lack of commitment is most publicly reflected in their unwillingness to take responsibility for the children they have fathered. This tendency in men to procreate but not care for their offspring is an old problem. It was the original tendency of most primate males. This behavior, sometimes referred to as the "male problematic," has many causes, some of which began with the industrial revolution. Laws that deduct child support from wages will insure the physical well-being of children, but those laws do not challenge the lack of commitment or the absence of responsibility of men toward the children they father. In the chapter on nurturing, we explore how men need to reverse the phenomenon of father absence and regard children as vulnerable persons of worth who need our protection and care. For this chapter, the focus is on helping men recover the virtue of promising.

There are many words we could use to describe the virtue of promising. *Commitment* is the more general term for bonding with others and maintaining that connection through acts of responsibility, self-giving, and loyalty. Most definitions of commitment are like promising because they emphasize persisting on a meaningful course of action or a relationship despite obstacles. Although there is overlap between committing and promising, promising is distinct because it is more interpersonal, more concrete, and more easily linked with the promises of God that precede all human promising. A promise is a pledge thrown ahead. One way to predict the future is to act on what we promise. Being responsible for something and being loyal to someone both imply that a promise has been made to act into the future in ways that will preserve and enhance a relationship. In this chapter I will use the verb "promising" rather than "keeping promises" in order to focus on this activity of making a commitment.

Promising is an ongoing human activity because the situations and obligations of our lives keep changing. It is not enough just to keep promises. The promises keep changing because the people change. As a result, many promises should not be kept in their original form. The paradox of promising again and again lies in the reality that the fulfillment of our promising often takes a different form than we imagined when we first pledged ourselves. This is certainly true in marriage. The people we think we are marrying turn out to be full of wonderful and complicated surprises. Even though men tend to think of themselves as a steady state, we change too. The secret to a vital marriage or a sustaining friendship is promising again and again in response to a changed situation. Even if men remain relatively constant, the future world of work is likely to include several career shifts over a lifetime. We are transformed as promise keepers when we reevaluate promises that are obsolete or renew the promises that endure. In that sense, we are always promising.[2]

Convictions are what make us dependable people when the odds are against us and we're tempted to cut and run. It is not where we take a stand that makes conviction a value, but that we do take a stand. . . . Heroism is not achieved by accomplishing a magnificent feat or losing one's life in a glorious battle. The test of conviction is in the ordinary affairs of life. . . . The finest belief system held without convictions produces instability and shallowness of character. Belief cannot produce character, unless it is backed by convictions that have been put to the test.

Ray S. Anderson,
Unspoken Wisdom: Truths My Father Taught Me

Promising is more than something humans do. It is a human virtue sustained by a promising God. Faith in a future that God continues to make new enables people to promise in the present. We have the courage to keep promising again and again because we believe the future toward which the whole creation is moving belongs to God. Our experience of God's faithfulness gives us strength to keep promising in the midst of human confusion and uncertainty. It took several encounters in the night before Jacob lived into the promises God had been making to him ever since he fled from home. We are not much different. Whether it is our pride or reluctance to acknowledge dependency and vulnerability that gets in the way, it takes a long time for men to acknowledge that God's loyalty makes our promising possible and necessary. Men deepening their faithfulness to God are promising persons.

IT MATTERS WHAT WE PROMISE

In recent years, one resource for men struggling to be faithful has been a movement called Promise Keepers, which highlights the importance of promising. Promise Keepers seeks to ignite, equip, and unite men "to keep the Seven Promises in and through involvement in the community of the local church." These promises provide content for the commitments men make to Jesus Christ, to other men, to their families, to racial justice, and to their local congregation. Although the rhetoric of the organization is problematic because it portrays God in a patriarchal way and the husband/father as the protector and upholder of authority in the family, Promise Keepers has made commitment a male issue and set high standards for what faithfulness means for Christian men. The perspective of this chapter differs from the emphasis of Promise Keepers in its focus on the verb "promising" rather than the noun "promise." People change and situations evolve; therefore simply keeping the promises we make is not sufficient. Because God continues to make all things new, being a promising person and the act of promising are as important as the promises themselves.

Promising is a process and an activity but there is also content to what we promise. In teaching pastoral care to future ministers, I have often said, "Do not promise what you cannot deliver." When a dying woman asked her pastor to take care of her fifty-year-old daughter who was moderately developmentally disabled, the pastor was in a tough spot. He did not know how to finesse this dying mother's request and so he made a promise he knew he could not keep. Two years later, the pastor is not involved but a handful of people from this small, struggling congregation are consumed by the responsibilities of caring for Yvonne. It is clear to everyone involved that without their care, Yvonne would be on the streets. For the pastor, it was a promise he should not have made because he could not keep it. We may make promises to get out of an uncomfortable situation only to discover that we are trapped by a promise we cannot possibly fulfill. In the moment, we intend no deceit. Promises are often made in good faith without counting the cost or considering the consequences.

Sometimes the promises we make are the result of cultural expectations for men: that men ought to keep the peace, fix a situation, or be the primary wage-earner. Rather than admit we do not fit the male mold, men will promise to fix the leaky toilet even when they have no clue about what needs to be done. The burden of being the provider for a family is a promise men are finding more difficult to keep in the new economic order. When men are trapped with too many responsibilities or commitments, they break promises or commitments they cannot keep rather than renegotiate the promise in the light of a changed situation. Thinking about oneself as a promise keeper will not help men assess situations in which a promise needs to be reevaluated before it is renewed.

If we decide to be a promising or committing person, we may have to decide between conflicting goods. In the account that begins this chapter, Jacob's promise to provide for the people of Israel was in conflict with his deep need to protect Benjamin, his beloved son with Rachel. The process of promising remains a virtue even when the content of our promises requires us to make difficult choices between competing goods. Eric enjoyed his work as a marketing analyst for a chain of department stores. He had been promoted several times since joining the company because of his commitments to work and the people who worked for him. When his oldest son, Kevin, scored the game winning run at a soccer match Eric could not attend, Eric began to rethink his priorities. Eric knew that his decision to spend more time with his three boys would have consequences for his advancement in the company, but he could no longer neglect his commitment to his family. They learned to live with less income so Eric could be more present in the family.

Modern marriages are often a constant juggling act of competing obligations and opportunities and conflicting commitments. Eric's decision to work less and spend more time with his family was a costly privilege. It was costly because his career was affected. It was a privilege because he could afford to work less and still support the family. Men who must work long hours at low wages to sustain a family financially often have little time to fulfill their commitments to wives and children. Even when fathers want to support their families, current economic trends make that harder and harder to do on a single low-paying job. Promising and promising again and again is only half the story. It also matters what we promise. For example, the promise to stay in a marriage or the desire to continue in a relationship is important but sometimes an empty promise unless it includes a commitment to improve the marital bond or relationship, sacrifice for it, invest in it, link personal goals to it, and seek the partner's welfare, not simply one's own.

What Prevents Men from Promising or Keeping Promises?

If the observation is accurate that the United States has become a low-commitment culture, women and men alike do not keep promises because they are part of a larger shift in values away from community and commitment and toward the individual and a desire to avoid loyalties that limit personal freedom. It is difficult not to be influenced by the trends in the culture. However, since this is a book about and for men, we also need to ask if there are particular male impediments to promising. What attitudes, habits, or social expectations must be set aside if men are to develop the practice of promising? As one way of exploring the issue, I have chosen sayings or slogans common to men that suggest barriers to promising. You will be able to add your own to this list.

I may not always be right, but I am never wrong. This was the winning maxim at a predominantly male gathering I attended some years ago. It is something that could have been said by Archie Bunker. Men sometimes persist in a certain way even when they know it is not right because they can never be wrong. Furthermore, if change is implied in promising again and again, letting go of old commitments no longer appropriate may seem like an admission that we were wrong before. When a friend of mine says, "Hey, I've got my reasons for what I'm doing," he is usually asserting his authority in order not to be challenged or buying time until he thinks of a good reason.

The relationship had outgrown its usefulness. We live in a society that is driven by cost effectiveness and contaminated by a utilitarian, disposable view of life and relationships. Such a view determines what is often referred to as "the bottom line." We keep commitments as long as they work for us. A relationship may outgrow the reason it began and hence diminishes because nothing new has emerged to reinvigorate the original commitment. Furthermore, if we are aware of the disposability of a relationship or wonder how long our usefulness to the company may last, we are reluctant to make long-term commitments in order to avoid hurt and embarrassment that looks like losing.

Winning is everything. Friendship is limited by competition. So are personal loyalties. In a society preoccupied with which team is number one or who is winning the competition for ratings or revenue, it is too easy to measure worth by winning rather than faithfulness. In a conversation about the effects of competition in this society, one student remembered a saying from his grandfather that had set the tone for his life. "For every bone, there are at least five dogs." His grandfather was a fierce competitor who looked at everything through the lens of winning or losing. If you want to win the bone, his grandfather would add, you have to know the competition. Promises are secondary to winning and commitments are calculated around knowing the competition.

I try not to get too close. That comment is often made in the corporate world where people are regarded as interchangeable parts. It has been observed that people who must flee from death will also flee from life. Commitments do end and relationships cannot last forever because people move away or die. The tragedy is that in order to flee from finitude and the awareness of death, we may run from life as well. We stop promising to avoid grief because love and grief come from the same source. Jack McCall, the central character in Pat Conroy's novel *Beach Music*, observes that because he grieves secretly, his love is hidden as well. The hidden river where love resides is like the inland sea of tears: it has no outlet. If love and grief flow from the same inland sea without outlet, it is not surprising that men love as indirectly as they grieve.[3]

You don't have to fix it. One consequence of being physically strong and responsible is that "fixing things" has been a social expectation of men and a standard male response to problems of any kind. Some things can be fixed but some things cannot. When husbands are encouraged by their wives to "listen without fixing," they are invited into powerlessness. The deeper challenge for men is to stay committed to a conversation or a relationship that cannot be fixed. Men are much too willing to walk away from situations in which they feel powerless. Men will be more likely to stay committed in powerless situations if they can add receptivity and waiting to their understanding of being human.

I need to take care of myself. In a highly individualistic society of affluence and choices, keeping a promise may be in direct conflict with the popular philosophy of self-care. The idea of sacrifice for the sake of keeping a promise often makes it difficult or even impossible to "have a life." Not long after they were married, Belinda Smith demanded that her husband, William, promise he would never put her in a nursing home. Now Belinda has Alzheimer's. In order for William to keep his promise, he does not have much of a life. His care of Belinda is full time and he does it without resentment. He wonders, however, when he will play golf again or count the offering after church. It is not a simple question. What happens when the promises we made long ago are too costly to keep today? How do we weigh our responsibilities toward others against our obligations to care for ourselves? Because women have traditionally been the designated family caregivers, these have not been questions for men in the past the way they have become critical issues for men in the present.

WHO'S IN CHARGE?

It is common for men to be less committed to activities, events, and relationships they are not in charge of. Or if the person in charge is incompetent, we are more inclined to compete for power than support his efforts to do the best he can. In recent years, men have struggled to accept greater equality between women and men in the workplace. Most men have made this transition easily. For men who have assumed that they are entitled to be in charge, the equality of women and men in the workplace has been difficult. One of the assumptions of patriarchy that has died hard is that men are entitled to be in charge. From some religious perspectives, it is still assumed a man is the "spiritual head" of the family. Headship of any kind presumes responsibility with or without power.

Over the last two hundred years, each generation of fathers has had less authority than the previous one. After the Industrial Revolution, the concept of fatherhood changed radically. Masculinity was no longer defined by fathering and husbanding in the home but by making money. When men had to leave home to work, their responsibility was to provide for the family by working outside the home.[4] Some men redefined this new situation by insisting that it was their nature to have this role of breadwinner. As women have joined the workforce with more equal pay for equal work, male assumptions of "headship through breadwinning" has had to change as well. For the last twenty years in our marriage, my wife has made the primary salary. Every time I tried to convince someone it did not bother me that I was not the primary breadwinner, I knew I was lying. While I do not believe it is my nature to be the family breadwinner, I had assumed I would have this responsibility. It was also an expectation that once defined my masculinity. The equation of money and power in this society has further complicated this shift in the role of family provider.

One of the constant themes in Jacob's life is a familiar struggle for modern men. Who we are and what we accomplish are both gift and achievement. We work hard, take responsibility seriously, and plan and strategize to achieve our goals in life, knowing all the while that all of life is a gift from God. St. Augustine, theologian of the early church, said that we are "to work as if all depends on you and pray as if all depends on God." It took a lifetime for Jacob to live into that promise. Our struggle is the same. Even though we need to work hard to support our families and fulfill our dreams, what we receive from our labors is all gift from God. It took several encounters with God in the night before Jacob came to understand this. Rabbi Michael Fishbane concludes his commentary on the Jacob story with these words: "No unpromised fire is stolen from heaven. To the contrary—those whom God has chosen succeed. But in the thickness of historical time, and because of limited divine interventions, realization of the divine promises appears to rest with human action."[5] What God promises, humans achieve.

A paradox exists in our commitments and our loyalties. Human promising is essential for community well-being and family vitality and yet human commitments are always qualified by our loyalty to God. There is always a deeper commitment to God that transcends human promising. Jesus used the division between parents and children to illustrate the conditions of discipleship. Over and over again, Jesus reminds us that family obligations are not the final aim of human life. We owe our families gratitude but not our souls. The same could be said for our commitments at work. Loyalty to our family and the workplace are necessary but cannot claim our unconditional loyalty. That belongs to God alone.

BEING A COMMITTING, PROMISING PERSON

Having convictions we can act on and being a committing kind of person are both characteristics of Christian faithfulness. I do not mean to imply that the content of that promise to follow Jesus does not matter. It does. But the content of that promise changes through the years as our understanding of Scriptures deepens and the commitment to discipleship is modified. Making a promise to be a committing person is not a simple thing, however. It is to be engaged in struggle with God and with the world. Being a committing person means that we engage in activities of faith even when we are not sure of the content of our belief. Being a committing person is one way to faithfulness.

Being a faithful, committed follower of God is more than what we do; it is about believing from the heart. For some men, that kind of faithfulness includes knowledge of theology and the traditions of the church. For other men, it is what Tex Sample has identified as "faith commitment from the heart." This kind of faith is "about a living trust that can sustain hard life in a world that does not come out right. Such a faith will be oriented toward survival, coping, need, belonging, and identity."[6] These are convictions that help men get up and go to work at jobs without promise. When these convictions are tested, they help to form character that endures. Such a sturdy faith sustains men through the dark nights of wrestling with strange dreams or visions that turn out in the morning to be angels of God. It will also lead us to worship with other struggling followers of God in order to be sustained in our life as committing, promising men of God. In between times of worship, our practice as promising people might be helped by these suggestions:

Keep the promises simple. Promising to be faithful, present, and truthful is difficult enough. We don't need to add more complexity. Sometimes when we make things complex, we are looking for reasons not to do it.

Make promises that are within our power to keep. It is within our power to be faithful. We cannot control the faithfulness of others nor can we anticipate how people might respond to our faithfulness. Being faithful does not depend on what others do.

It is within our power to be present. Being present is more than showing up. You may be at your daughter's basketball game and spend half of the time in the lobby on your cell phone. Being present requires a commitment to attentiveness.

It is within our power to be truthful. There was a time when a man was as good as his word. We could assume that a man's word was good, that signed documents prepared by lawyers and witnessed by a notary were not necessary to be sure that someone would keep a promise or fulfill an agreement.

Be prepared to acknowledge our failure. We will break promises and fail to keep commitments. Sometimes the situation creates the failure. Other times, it is selfishness or sloth that prevents us from keeping a promise. The willingness to acknowledge a failed commitment and a clear intent to make the necessary adjustments in one's life pattern so it is less likely to happen again are part of learning the practice of promising. Reconciliation is part of promising.

God's utter loyalty makes fragile human promising possible. Because a promise is a pledge thrown ahead, it requires us to trust the future as a gracious mystery. It is a risk sustained by the belief that we can trust the future because it belongs to God. Becoming committing persons depends in large part on trusting the graciousness of God, whose promises are for us and before us. Because the church supports men who make and break promises, it is the singularly most important context in our society to help men through this time of transition. The development of men's ministries that emphasize God's promises of grace and forgiveness will help men move through this time to a new sense of mutuality between women and men, between men and men, and with God.

PAYING ATTENTION

There were times in the life of Jacob when he did not seem to be paying attention to anyone or anything else but his own interests. He was so focused on a goal that he overlooked other things happening in his life. For example, his strong desire to have Rachel as his wife made it easy for Laban to trick Jacob into marrying his other daughter, Leah. Jacob and his family were on a journey to a new home when his beloved Rachel died giving birth to Benjamin. Although he built a pillar at her grave, there is no report of Jacob's lament. Instead, we are told that "Israel journeyed on, and pitched his tent before the tower of Eder" (Gen. 35:21). When Jacob's daughter Dinah was raped by Shechem, the son of a local leader, Jacob was less attentive to the violation of his daughter than he was fearful that the local inhabitants might attack him and destroy his household (see Gen. 34:30). At the end of his life, however, when Jacob gave blessings to his twelve sons, the specificity of those blessings or the absence of blessing gave evidence that Jacob had been paying attention to the behavior of his sons.

God was able to get Jacob's attention through dramatic encounters. In possession of a stolen blessing and in flight from Esau's revenge, Jacob had a dream on his way to his uncle Laban's land that confirmed the presence of God with Jacob despite his treachery. "Then Jacob woke from his sleep and said, 'Surely the Lord is in this place—and I did not know it'" (Gen. 28:16). When he was with Laban, however, Jacob was preoccupied with getting the wife he wanted and amassing wealth. Jacob needed another reminder of God's presence. This occurred when Jacob wrestled in the night with an unknown assailant (whom Jacob later declared was God) on his way to meet Esau. Again, Jacob was frightened. There is a rhythm to Jacob's awareness of God's presence in his life that is familiar to men. During the day, Jacob's decisions are self-centered and intent on mastery or success. God waited to appear to Jacob at night when he was less preoccupied and more vulnerable. It was in the night that Jacob learned about attending to the mystery of God's initiating presence in his life.

Hebrew Bible scholars suggest that Jacob was the first human being to pray at night. Until Jacob, "praying in the dark" had been an impossible act of faith. When Jacob was able to leave all support systems behind, he moved into the world of the night where nothing is clear, all is shifting, phantasm, illusion. It was here, paradoxically, that Jacob found his ground of truth. Sleep seemed to be the basic condition for God's revelation. In his sleep, Jacob was not aware of himself and therefore not engaged in the conscious act of developing his relation to God. He was able to recognize God's presence because he was not preoccupied with achieving his goals. This account of Jacob's life is common to men today who are preoccupied with stocks and bonds, the price of hogs, struggling with living alone, managing two jobs to make ends meet, or living with a secret. When it is night and men are not so absorbed with their lives, they are more likely to attend to the presence of God.

There are very few men who have not heard someone say to them, "You're not paying attention." I would usually hear those words when I tried to watch a basketball game on television and read a book while my daughter, son, or wife wanted to tell me something. I thought I was mostly listening to them but they were very clear that I was not paying attention. And they were correct. The other sentence men often hear is, "Did you hear anything I said?" For me, that question is usually asked when I try to give the appearance of paying attention even though I am doing something else at the same time. In truth, I am preoccupied and not paying attention. The common response of men is to say something defensive like, "I was listening. It's just that I have a lot on my mind." The implicit message, hardly ever said, is that what men have on their minds is more important than anything wives or children have to say.

Children are quick to remind fathers when they are not paying attention and wives can regularly attest to the experience of being looked over romantically and then overlooked in marriage. Men can oversee clearly at work but they do not see the new furniture arrangement in the living room. While no father would admit he values pro football or college basketball's March Madness more than he values his children or wife, behavior suggests otherwise. The troubling reality behind the absence of recognition in the family is that paying attention is a selectively developed practice that men reserve for people and things they value most.

According to Dave Barry, men, or rather *guys*, are capable of tremendous visual concentration but they have little control over what their eyeballs choose to concentrate on, which means they are inclined to miss certain subtle details, like what their wives look like. Whether or not Barry is correct about male anatomy and the control of eyeballs, he is painfully accurate in describing the inability to see clearly even those they love the most.

> Take the case of a couple I know named (really) Steele and Bobette Reeder. One time Bobette was getting ready to substantially change her hairstyle, and, in a gesture of compassion, she decided to alert Steele.
>
> "Steele," she said. "You never notice when I change my hair, so this time I'm telling you ahead of time: I'm going to get a new hairstyle today. It's going to look completely different."
>
> So that evening, when Steele got home from work, he immediately started raving about how nice Bobette's hair looked, how much better he liked it, etc. He was so excited about her new hairstyle that she had to interrupt him to say: "Steele, they canceled my appointment."[1]

This reluctance to pay attention is not a genetic deficiency in men. Nor is it a male variation of attention deficit disorder. Because men have dominated positions of leadership for centuries, they have been encouraged to see the big picture and develop long-term plans. As a result, men have tended to overlook what is near at hand. The kind of visionary thinking that has preoccupied men makes a ready excuse for overlooking those close by. We reward men who have a single-minded focus on one goal or one achievement or who are consumed by their career. In order to achieve their goals, attending to the task to get the work done has been the priority for men more than attending to people.

The determination to achieve a goal and the responsibility or desire to hold a wider vision also have consequences for the spiritual life of men. Paying attention to God and paying attention to others around us require the same disposition, one that needs to be developed in men. There is a connection between paying attention to those who are near and Christian faithfulness in at least two respects: (1) Men who seek to be faithful to God in daily living will want to show respect for others by paying attention at home and at work; and (2) When men are willing to recognize others, we are also more likely to receive the gifts others have to give. In the biblical tradition, that kind of hospitality to the gifts of others may eventuate in welcoming angels without knowing it (see Heb. 13:1–2). Because recognition is such a fundamental human need, men will need to develop new forms of attentiveness that will enable them to see more clearly those near at hand like wives, children, and co-workers.

In this chapter, we will examine the importance of paying attention in three distinct ways: first, learning to attend more carefully to those we love; second, seeing the strangers in our midst as unique gifts from God, who may be angels without our knowing it; and third, attending to the presence of God in our lives, which means listening to the sound of thunder or riveting dramas of transformation. Attending to God also means attending to the still, small voice of a dream, enduring sleepless struggles in the night, or heeding the lonely cry of a stranger. Regarding ourselves as persons of worth with dignity and deserving respect makes it possible to attend to others and to God . We will also be more likely to pay attention to others if we acknowledge that human beings cannot thrive without recognition.

THE HUMAN NEED FOR RECOGNITION

The need for recognition is basic. We never outgrow the need for recognition that begins in the interaction between a newborn child and its mother. The growth of a self depends on the recognition by people we also recognize and whose recognition we eventually value. The philosopher Descartes coined the popular maxim "I think, therefore I am" to reinforce this view that the self is formed from the inside out. The English psychiatrist D. W. Winnicott turned that saying into a slightly different principle that in turn reflects the human need for recognition at a deeper level: "I am seen, therefore I am." Being recognized is a risky dimension of a process that includes contradiction and paradox. We want to be emotionally free and self-determined and yet we desperately want to be recognized by the same people from whom we want to be free. This intimacy paradox posed by our simultaneous need for recognition and independence applies in friendship and marriage alike.

At the beginning of human life, a self is filled up through the recognition and adoration of nurturing individuals who provide a mirror for the emerging person. Adoring parents, grandparents, and others fill up a self by responding to the infant's positive, developmental need for recognition. As a grandfather, I have permission to spend hours watching my grandchildren play, draw, eat, and even sleep. When children do not receive adequate recognition and mirroring in infancy for whatever reason, the self is impoverished. The self is a problem in our time because this recognition is in short supply. As a result of this internal poverty of the self, it is difficult to maintain an inner core of identity in the face of external stress. Attending to another human being is a universal human obligation that begins the formation of a self.

We come to life through the attention of others. The recognition we receive from them is not only life enhancing, it is also life creating, and that is why it is so important that the attention we give another is love. There are people dying for attention, people silently screaming out for a moment of recognition, a chance to be befriended.

Paul J. Waddell, *Friendship and the Moral Life*

The process of forming a male self has a special complexity that affects the capacity for mutual recognition later in life. We have learned from Carol Gilligan and others after her what we probably already knew: that the selves of women and the selves of men are formed differently. "Since masculinity is defined through separation while femininity is defined through attachment, male gender identity (i.e., the male self) is threatened by intimacy while female gender identity (i.e., the female self) is threatened by separation."[2] If men achieve a sense of self by separating from the mutuality of the primary bond, we should not be surprised that men have difficulty paying attention to others in later life. If the separate or autonomous self is the norm, then it is easy for men to absolve themselves from relationships or the necessity of recognition.

In the translator's introduction to *The Struggle for Recognition* by Axel Honneth, Joel Anderson wrote: "The conditions for self-realization turn out to be dependent on the establishment of relationships of mutual recognition. These relationships go beyond (a) close relations of love and friendship to include (b) legally institutionalized relations of universal respect for the sake of autonomy and dignity of persons, and (c) networks of solidarity and shared values within which the particular worth of individual members of a community can be acknowledged."[3] What is particularly significant about that quotation for this chapter is that the responsibility for providing communities of recognition goes beyond the family and most certainly includes communities of faith. If congregations are to be communities of mutual recognition, men need to increase their ability to pay attention as an act of Christian faithfulness.

SIGHS OF AN UNDERNOURISHED SOUL

Even when men think they have moved beyond old stereotypes of masculinity that celebrate the separate male self at the expense of human communities, we discover patterns of behavior in men, like not paying attention, that are residues of a time we thought we had left behind. Certainly in this society and probably still in churches, men regularly set aside the connective aspects of the communal self in favor of the freedom and self-assertion of the separate self. Human fullness, of course, is both. To be free and self-determined selves, men need to be simultaneously autonomous and connected to others through communities of mutual recognition.

Persons of all ages and occupations must deal with the Attachment/Separateness polarity. If we become too separate, our contact with the world is lost and our capacity for survival jeopardized. If we become too attached to the environment, we endanger our capacity for self-renewal, growth and creative effort. Although a balance of attachment and separateness must be found at every age, it will necessarily change from one era of the life cycle to the next.

Daniel J. Levinson, *The Seasons of a Man's Life*

The psychologist C. G. Jung is reported to have said it this way: "Only paradox comes anywhere near to comprehending the fullness of human life." For that reason, the complex and sometimes painful struggles of our time to think about being a man in ways that unite rather than divide will take us inevitably to paradox and process. The self is not a fixed substance we possess but a process in time. The self owns its world but cannot hoard the gain. At any moment, the self is clearly distinguishable (or needs to be) *as* itself and then in the next moment departs from its own selfness to be in community. The self is bounded and permeable, separate and attached. It is imminent in the community and connected with the earth and yet at the same time the self transcends itself, takes risks, and knows itself as object. It is the same old self and always new. That is the paradox of self.

When this delicate contradiction between the separate and communal self is not maintained, recognition is diminished and the self is depleted. If we do not belong to communities of mutual recognition, we are an unrecognized self. The self becomes depleted when the ordinary and necessary human needs for recognition are unmet. We may never have thought about ourselves as depleted, but we may have used words like empty, exhausted, drained, demoralized, deflated, bereft, needy, and starving to describe our experience as men in a difficult time. These are the deep hungers of the self and express the inarticulate sighs of an undernourished soul. The self is a social reality, within rather than apart from communities of mutual recognition. When men are unable to form communities that will fill this deeper, inner experience of depletion, they will also be less likely to provide the kind of recognition that will nourish the selves of others. The biblical language of covenant most clearly conveys the relationship between the person as an individual moral agent and the communities of obligation or common cause within which each individual agent grows and thrives if he is known and recognized by people who matter.

PAYING ATTENTION TO THOSE WE LOVE

Marriages that endure and flourish and children who thrive and grow depend on a kind of mutual recognition in which each honors the other as a separate and unique subject worthy of respect. In an essay entitled "On Love and Other Difficulties," Rainer Maria Rilke described the kind of recognition that is necessary in order to sustain marriage over time. "Once the realization is accepted that even between the closest human beings infinite distances continue to exist, a wonderful living side by side can grow up, if they (the couple) succeed in loving the distance between them which makes it possible for each to see the other whole and against a wide sky."[4] Distance makes intimacy possible even though it does not guarantee it will happen. Living side by side enhances community but it does not always lead to seeing the other clearly. Sometimes we only see an intimate partner as a project to improve or an object to use. Even if each partner in marriage is a clearly defined self, mutual recognition of the uniqueness by each partner is necessary for a marriage or other relationship to endure.

Recognition is a prelude to mutual respect. It occurs when we take seriously the thoughts and feelings and intentions of someone we care about, even if we do not understand them. When each partner in an intimate relationship sees the particular gifts and hopes of the other, domination is diminished and the possibility of equality is increased. In marriage, men have not always paid close attention either to their wives or their children. Men may be so preoccupied with their worlds of work or play that the people they are closest to are overlooked or taken for granted. Jefferson Butler had been married for nineteen years when Roselyn, his wife, received a service award for her work as a nurse. At the banquet, things were said about her gifts and abilities that Jefferson had not known. What amazed him, Jefferson told me, was how little he had known and yet had not looked. The darkest side of this pattern in men is that we are curious about what we value. If we do not value the gifts, intellect, and abilities of the women we love, then it is easy not to know and not to look. For most men, however, not paying attention to those we love is about being preoccupied with other things.

Archie Logan is a physician in a small town in England in Joanna Trollope's novel *A Passionate Man*. He has a successful medical practice, an overlooked wife, three children, an aging father whom he adores, and very few friends. Liza, his wife, decides to return to teaching, his father marries again, and land developers threaten to upset their quiet village. As Archie's life unravels, so does the marriage. Most of all, Liza wanted Archie to recognize her, recognize that she had changed, that things do not always stay as they have been.

> She said, in as gentle a voice as she could manage, "You speak to me as if my point of view couldn't possibly have the validity of yours because I'm me and you are you and all that that implies. Why can't you speak to me with the courteous interest you speak with to other people?"
>
> Archie said, "I was under the impression that I was being perfectly polite. And of course I am interested in what you think. I just don't think you have thought far enough or widely enough."
>
> "And I," said Liza, "think you are a pompous prig."[5]

Later on, when Archie tried to make up, he insisted that he "esteemed" Liza. She had changed and he did not know what to do about it.

What Liza learned from that painful conversation was confirmation of what she had always suspected. Archie loved her but did not regard her as an equal.

Perhaps there are very few Archie Logans among men today, but the inability to pay attention to those we love is rooted in part in practices derived from a time when men like Archie Logan were the male norm. When we realize how difficult it is to see those we love "whole and against a wide sky," men may begin to realize why we miss the gifts of strangers. In order to correct the male inclination to overlook those we love, we may need to begin by listening to birds, noting a hillside of daffodils, and listening for the presence of God in our nighttime struggles in order to practice paying attention.

What is necessary for marriage and other intimate relationships is also necessary in relating to children. The experience of being recognized is not only a prerequisite for intimacy and community; it is fundamental, as we have said, for human development. When we are too busy to hear a child's story or see a new drawing or when we forget to pick up a daughter from soccer practice or do not attend a son's school play, we unintentionally diminish a child's sense of worth. Again, the determination to pay attention depends on our attitude toward others. If husbands would regard their wives as equal partners and if fathers regarded their children as fully human and of equal worth, there would be fewer instances of domestic violence and child abuse and fewer troubled children.

PAYING ATTENTION TO DIFFERENCE

For the last fifteen years of my teaching, I was in a school where a large number of students came from outside the United States. In almost every class, I would have as many as ten different cultures of the world present. The "church catholic" or universal church was regularly visible to me. That diversity made teaching richer and more complex. I needed to pay attention to differences every day. It is not enough to say that the planet has shrunk because of technology that has made travel and communication easy and instantaneous. Cultures of the world have dispersed. Encounters with diversity that once were the province of missionaries, the adventurous, the open-minded, and those too poor to live where they wished are an unavoidable and irreversible part of the landscape of daily living. The diversity of the world is increasingly part of our workplaces and the family table. I have a son-in-law whose family came from Puerto Rico and a daughter-in-law born in the Netherlands. My grandson, Jonah, who is three, is learning English and Dutch at the same time. My granddaughter, Julia, will learn Spanish from one grandmother.

Honoring difference has never been so easy and it is still difficult. We have often divided the world between *us* and *them*. The impulse to determine who is *in* and who is *out*, who belongs to the family and who *does not*, who is *us* and who *them* has had as its larger aim determining identity and belonging. We continue to say that we belong with people who are like us. People who are not like us are outsiders. When the person we have decided is "the outsider" becomes my employee, doctor, neighbor, or daughter's husband, then learning to live with difference is no longer optional. It is necessary for human survival. In order to understand people we meet who are culturally, racially, or ethnically different, we need to learn to honor diversity.

Ethnic and racial tension in our time is a consequence of many complex and sometimes conflicting emotions. Too much difference in our neighborhoods and churches may be perceived as dangerous for men who grew up believing that sameness is the way to safety. Men who fear that they will eventually lose their jobs because of preferential hiring resent diversity. For other men, there is a close connection between prejudice and intolerance of ambiguity. Cultural differences create uncertainty about human behavior. Men who are intolerant of ambiguity are likely to feel threatened by difference and react negatively. In contrast, "a person who is tolerant of ambiguity does not experience ambiguous situations as threatening and may even view them as desirable."[6] If this assessment of one origin of prejudice is accurate, learning to live with ambiguity becomes a necessary dimension of Christian faithfulness for the common good.

There is yet one other source of our difficulties with difference. In his book *Escape from Evil*, Ernest Becker connected the fear of death and violence toward those who are different.[7] In order to gain a sense of immortality against the dread of death, human beings persecute some and dominate others. It is an ancient pattern that men know well: we make ourselves taller by standing on the bodies of others. Outsiders, aliens, those who are lazy or do not belong are devalued and abused to feed our need for omnipotent feelings and a sense of self-importance. We look for scapegoats to kick to feel special. The fear of being small prompts bullies to pick on high school nerds in order to make themselves more important. If violence toward others is driven by the inability to accept our creatureliness, difference, and the inevitability of death, then learning to live with vulnerability becomes a moral imperative in order to live responsibly and justly in a diverse creation.

Whenever we encounter someone who invites us to see the world in a new way, there is the possibility of being transformed. That is the gift of difference. Learning to honor difference without fear occurs when we have a personal experience with someone whose difference enlarges our vision of the human and transforms our attitude toward the stranger. Such an encounter with difference jolts us out of the presumption that *"our world is the world"* and invites us to expand our vision of life to include something new. The self is transformed as it is enlarged to include the stranger with different gifts. Hospitality is the action by which we honor the gifts of any other human being. Because hospitality is a metaphor for the gospel, it is also a norm for Christian faithfulness.

PAYING ATTENTION TO GOD BY WELCOMING THE STRANGER

Hospitality is a human necessity because diversity is an increasing reality in our neighborhoods, churches, and homes. Hospitality is a Christian virtue because it is the sign of a gracious God who always welcomes us, creating space for us to live our story. When we welcome a stranger to our home or honor a child added to our family, we do the same. The stranger has a story to tell or a gift to give that has the power to expand our understanding of the world. Sometimes, the stranger is very close at hand. Husbands and wives, for example, honor one another's uniqueness by welcoming the personal changes that inevitably occur over the years of a marriage.

One of the consequences of not paying close attention to that which is near at hand in our lives is that we may miss the presence of God. Although hospitality has been regarded largely as woman's work, it is a human practice of receptivity by means of which we show respect to others and through which communities of mutual recognition are formed. Long ago, when hospitality was a necessary way of life, it was Jacob's grandfather Abraham who welcomed three strangers to his tent one day and was given the promise of a son. While it is certainly true that some strangers are dangerous, human life is impoverished when we use difference to keep others at distance. Kosuke Koyama, a Japanese theologian, once observed that the only way to stop the conflict and violence among and between people in our world is by practicing hospitality to strangers where we live and where we work.[8] Being hospitable is an undeveloped practice for men that will only be fostered by being intentionally welcoming, receptive, and attentive.

When we welcome the stranger, we may unwittingly entertain angels. We also need to be open to the presence of God. God's presence is often more like a surprise attack than the result of sustained summons or longing. Encounters with God do not always occur in the fullness of selfhood and light but rather in the night when we are vulnerable. Jacob spoke for many men when he said after his dream that "the Lord is in this place and I did not know it." We are most likely to be surprised by God if we are able to leave a crack in our defenses. According to Hebrew Rabbinic tradition, that is why God appeared to Jacob in the night: his defenses were down. Men who regard most relationships as competitive in one way or another cannot afford to leave any doors ajar. If there are no windows of vulnerability, if our door to the world is never ajar, we are not likely to be surprised by God.

When the door to the soul is slightly open or ajar, God does not need to wait to enter. The door ajar is another image of vulnerability and hospitality. Leaving the door ajar is the gift of a distracted soul. It is the consequence of persisting in the struggle toward faithfulness as men. Leaving the door slightly open is possible when we are no longer preoccupied with defending ourselves from unseen enemies. If there is no door open, we will end up keeping God waiting much too long. Like Jacob, men today may need to pray in the night when no one will see our vulnerability. If we pray long enough at night, eventually we will learn to live with a crack in our defenses so that God might surprise us during daylight. Leaving the door of our lives ajar, we can never be sure who or what will come in. Moreover, it is possible that an encounter with a stranger will take us to the presence of God.

NURTURING

The meeting with Esau that Jacob has feared since he left Laban is about to happen. Jacob is traveling with his family and with cattle, sheep, and goats, some of which are very young. When he sees Esau and four hundred men coming toward him, he rearranges his entourage so that those who are closest to him are farther in the back in case there is conflict. Jacob's fear evaporates when he sees and hears the spontaneous welcome from Esau. There is no reference to Jacob's past trickery or Esau's promised revenge. The joy of two brothers meeting in peace is like Jacob's mysterious but gracious encounter with God. Jacob, who had very recently struggled with God, compares Esau's reception to "seeing the face of God" (Gen. 33:10). The forgiveness is sealed when Esau accepts the gifts Jacob has brought.

> Then Esau said, "Let us journey on our way, and I will go alongside you." But Jacob said to him, "My lord knows that the children are frail and that the flocks and herds, which are nursing, are a care to me; and if they are

overdriven for one day, all the flocks will die. Let my lord
pass on ahead of his servant, and I will lead on slowly,
according to the pace of the cattle that are before me and
according to the pace of the children, until I come to my
lord in Seir." (Gen. 33:11–14)

Eventually Esau and Jacob decide to travel separately to their
destination. Jacob's awareness that the children travel more
slowly is a sign of a parent's nurturing heart.

Jacob's heart was broken many times by the behavior of his
sons. Nothing, however, was more painful than the loss of Joseph,
whom he loved more than any of his other children. When Jacob
is tricked by his sons into believing that Joseph had been
devoured by wild animals (Gen. 37:33), he wept for many days
and refused to be comforted. When Jacob was asked to send his
youngest son, Benjamin, to Egypt in order to receive food for his
people suffering famine, Jacob refused. "My son shall not go
down with you, for his brother [Joseph] is dead, and he alone is
left" (Gen. 42:38). If he were to lose another son in his old age,
the sorrow would consume Jacob. Every parent who has lost a
child understands Jacob's fierce determination not to lose
another child.

The story of Jacob is about a lifelong struggle to be faithful to
God's vision for the people of Israel. It is also about a man
determined to be a responsible father. Being a father was seldom
easy for Jacob. Having twelve boys to raise meant he had more
than his share of heartache. Sometimes, however, Jacob seems
insensitive to the internal needs of his family. When his daughter
Dinah was raped by Shechem, Jacob overlooked the violation of
his daughter and the violent revenge by his sons because he was
more fearful that the local inhabitants might attack him and
destroy his household. Modern fathers might be appalled by
Jacob's insensitivity and that of his sons (murder does not repair
rape) until we remember the times when we too sacrificed family
well-being for some external threat or pressure.

There are two themes in this exploration about being a father: one,
that men recognize the responsibility and privilege of nurturing their
children; and two, that fathers particularly commit to forming sons who

will embrace new, more responsive ways of being a man. While each father today has a unique story about his relationship to his children, there are several predictable life-cycle moments in a child's life that require a father's best effort: welcoming a child, raising a child, blessing a child, letting a child go, making a child a friend. How men respond as fathers to these challenges will be shaped by their willingness to embrace nurturing as an aspect of manliness.

THE NEED FOR NURTURING FATHERS

This chapter is about the many meanings of nurturing. I have chosen the broader category of nurturing (rather than fathering) because it invites men to explore ways to foster growth in others at work and church as well as at home; it acknowledges that men in second marriages nurture children they did not biologically father; and it avoids gender restrictions around the care of children for all kinds of families. Nurture is any activity that nourishes and sustains life. In its most basic expression, nurture includes the provision of whatever is necessary to help any living organism grow and flourish. Although it is possible to foster human growth under traumatic or even dangerous circumstances, clean air and water and a safe environment certainly enhance nurturing. Nurture is what we naturally do when we care for people we love but it may also include intentional efforts to make a garden grow, foster a client relationship, or support a friend's growth. Fathers nurture when they attend to the well-being and growth of their sons and daughters.

Not all fathers, however, nurture growth in their children. In his book *Fatherless America*, David Blankenhorn identifies the absence of fathers as our most urgent social problem. Not only are fathers absent, society has a culturally impoverished conception of fatherhood closely resembling what Blankenhorn refers to as the "unnecessary father."[1] Boys who have no fathers to guide them into manhood must learn about being a man from other sources. When Louis W. Sullivan was secretary of the U.S. Department of Health and Human Services, he suggested that we are raising a generation of young males, to the peril of us all, who measure their manhood by the caliber of their gun. We need to shift our attention to male responsibility and the role that fathers play in raising children. What we have identified elsewhere as the "male problematic" (that men do not take responsibility for the children they procreate) should be a matter of great concern when men gather to think and pray about changes we must make.

Although absent or preoccupied fathers are a complex problem for our time, it is not society's only dilemma regarding the family. Nor is it the main thrust of this chapter. Our primary focus is on men and fathers nurturing children. Men have assumed for a long time that nurturing is something women do. As a result, nurturing is an underdeveloped practice in men. Even proposals about restoring the role of fathering presume that parenting is a gender specific activity: children need fathers to challenge them to climb higher and take more risks and they need mothers to nurture them and soothe the hurts they get from climbing higher. The assumption that men do not nurture naturally or may even be incapable of nurture has unnecessarily and inappropriately confined parenting roles for fathers.

> Our society is sending men mixed messages. It tells them that their children are the most important thing in their lives, yet marginalizes them if they put their families first. Given such conflicting signals, it's hardly surprising that men aren't eager to take on more parenting duties.
> Ellis Cose, *A Man's World: How Real Is Male Privilege—And How High Is Its Price?*

In contrast to these limiting perspectives on men, I am awed by the way my son and my son-in-law nurture their children. They relate to my grandchildren with patience, wonder, and respect. They delight in the gifts of their children. They willingly alter their own plans or desires to respond to the needs of their children. My son-in-law is the primary parent. My son and daughter-in-law share the parenting responsibility equally. For them, there is no predetermined dichotomy between what fathers do and what mothers do. Decisions about parenting responsibilities can be made more freely and fairly. In a 1998 interview for the public radio program *Ideas and Issues*, my son, Joel Anderson, made these observations in support of just and equal coparenting:

> There are studies that suggest that fathers and mothers tend to interact with their children in different ways: fathers, it is claimed, tend to engage in more active play with kids. *Dad winds the kids up, and Mom calms them down.* Dad's active play gets the kids all excited. The kids love it. But then, like clockwork, the children get so wound up that they don't know what to do with themselves anymore. Suddenly they are cranky and Dad doesn't know what to do so he passes them to Mom. This is obviously not a lot of fun for Mom. So the question arises: if fathers did not have mothers around to pass cranky children, would they be as likely to wind kids up. I don't think so.

This has consequences for justice in child care responsibilities. It gives fathers the high-excitement time that kids love and burdens mothers with the temper tantrum. If we divide parenting into mothers engaged in supporting, nurturing, and calming, and fathers engaged in active play, exploring, and teaching, then one parent responds to crises and the other pushes them beyond the comfort zone. Which of these can more easily be done according to the parent's schedule? Clearly the father's. You can postpone peek-a-boo or a trip to the zoo much more easily than you can postpone comforting a wailing child or making food for a hungry kid.[2]

This perspective is an alternative to those who continue to insist that fathering and mothering are gender-determined practices in the family. These changes are already occurring in many families. However, it is still very easy for women and men alike to revert to old defined roles for parenting that implicitly carry these expressions of injustice. Ultimately, it is not an issue of gender particularity. Even if it were to be established that women and men parent differently, we would need to attend to patterns of parenting that unintentionally foster an unjust distribution of difficult responsibility. As the following incident illustrates, the changes occurring in parenting practices are not without tension or emotional pain.

Ben was playing softball and his wife stopped by after work to find out whether he had fed the baby. "Hey mommy on second base," yelled the umpire, "did you feed your baby yet?" The otherwise easygoing Ben yelled back to his wife from second base: "No. And don't ask me that question in public again—just feed the baby."

Both the culture and the legal climate that enable child care and homemaking responsibilities to be shared equally are changing slowly. Even so, more fathers have primary responsibility for the care of their own children. Homosexual partners must raise their children without recourse to traditional gender divisions. Men in second marriages are expected to further the growth of stepchildren even though they are not their fathers. Some men in second marriages have developed patterns of coparenting between the absent birth father and the resident stepfather to avoid canny child manipulation or confusing double messages from two caring men. The use of nurturing that is inclusive of fathering broadens the range of caregivers. It also connects nurturing people with nurturing the land.

Husbandry as Nurturing

Children and relationships are not all that men nurture. The word "husbandry," from which we get husband, comes from the Old English word *husbanda* and the Old Norse *bua* that means "dwell." A husband was a household dweller bonded to his home and land instead of being a wanderer or nomad. Husbandry is the vocation of managing the resources of creation wisely. In this sense, to be a man or husband means to care for the place one has been entrusted with. One consequence of the Industrial Revolution is that men have been alienated from both their families and the earth. They have lost direct awareness of what it means to steward the land and care for families. Husbandry implies the sober and measured allocation of human and nonhuman resources for the future of generations.

Being a husbandman means making commitments and putting down roots. Anthony B. Robinson made this connection with husbandry in the newsletter of Plymouth Congregational Church in Seattle. Rather than berating men as oppressors or outlaws, he wrote, we may do better by encouraging them to consider "the deep role and tasks of husbandry, of husbanding or cultivating a new generation, caring for families and for public life . . . and building the household of humanity." I agree. Because men have lost their connection to the earth and the rhythms of creation, it is easy to neglect responsibility to husband the earth. As a result, the whole planet is in peril. Reclaiming husbandry as a metaphor for men will change how we care for the earth for the sake of our children and their children. Husbandry also introduces an alternative vision of time in contrast to the magical speed of modern technology that affects nurturing.

Magician is one ancient image of maleness. According to Robert Moore, "shamans, medicine men, wizards, witch doctors, brujos, inventors, scientists, doctors, lawyers, technicians—all these are accessing the same masculine energy pattern, no matter what age or culture they live in."[3] Among other things, the Magician is the master of technology. Men's identities since the Industrial Revolution have been linked to being technical "magicians" who manipulate the resources of creation to manufacture a world. A magician depends on cleverness to create an artificial situation or a compelling illusion in which speed and mastery dominate. Fax machines, orbiting satellites, and instant access to almost anything are part of a technology that has altered how we think about time.

Because we have come to expect not to wait, we have little practice at patience. Nurture is difficult if we always hurry. In the world of baseball, for example, the process of developing a young pitcher with a great arm cannot be rushed, however much a major league team might need his talent. Many boys have had to become men too soon because their fathers died young or because they went to war or their parents divorced. In recent time, impatient parents who push their children to grow up too soon have forgotten that it takes time and patience to nurture growth that endures. When parents are impatient, children are hurried.

David Horsey, a syndicated cartoonist for the *Seattle Post-Intelligencer*, created a painfully accurate picture of parental impatience titled "An American Childhood." Surrounded by books, a young boy is working away at a kitchen table while his mother talks on the phone. "I'm sorry, Billy, Johnny's got four hours of homework . . . tomorrow, there's soccer . . . swimming lessons . . . math tutor . . . Tai Bo on Tuesdays . . . science camp this weekend . . . Japanese lessons . . . piano . . . ah! I think he can squeeze you in for a half hour of chasing frogs in the pond two weeks from Sunday!"[4]

Because parents have prematurely imposed their adult view of time, the freedom of childhood is lost. The recovery of more unstructured time for children depends on the willingness of parents to be patient with the speed of a child's growth and be willing to wait while children decide how to use their free time.

In this society, and perhaps particularly for men, waiting is difficult to do. Men in particular are inclined to think of being active and in control as power. By contrast, waiting feels more like helplessness, powerlessness, and passivity. Violence toward children is sometimes the result of impatience with the inability of children to speak up or walk fast. This reluctance to wait has been reinforced by digital technology. If efficiency is the measure of all things, then it should not be surprising that children, the elderly, and the handicapped present a challenge to a society that is preoccupied with speed. We will be more effective in nurturing our children as fathers if we practice waiting.

Although it may be possible to manipulate the growth of cucumbers or nasturtiums, watching things grow ordinarily takes patience. Those who have a garden understand when I suggest that we consider *gardener* as an alternative to the image of *magician* because it invites us to think about the nurturing dimension of being a man. Like husbandry, the metaphor of being a gardener fosters virtues like gentleness, patience, and feeling connected to the earth, essential aspects of a spirituality of nurturing. Everything takes time to grow. One can only nurture, wait, and weed a little to be sure the environment is uncluttered or safe enough to promote growth. If a dominant male metaphor is husbandry or gardener, being a man might include tending the places where we live, making gardens where we can, connecting to the earth, and establishing the timetables of our life according to how cucumbers mature and nasturtiums blossom more than how fax machines work.

FATHERS WHO NURTURE

Practices of parenting previously excluded from our understanding of being a man (except in unusual circumstances) are now included in an increasingly expanded vision of manhood. For example, fathers change diapers, do the four o'clock feeding, walk their children to kindergarten, and do the evening pick-up after ballet practice. It is seldom said anymore that fathers "baby-sit" their children. In fact, a father may be the primary parent for an interval because of a mother's commitment or on a permanent basis because the mother is the primary wage earner. As the primary parent, my son-in-law has learned all the things one must be attentive to as a parent to foster the safety and well-being of a child. Because this expanded role is so new, there are not ready metaphors for fathers who are the primary parent. We call him the "at-home Dad."

> In the more than a dozen years I have been a father, I have been stirred to every imaginable parental feeling—raised to ecstasy by my children's sensitivity and generosity, and ashamed by their greed and jealousy; encouraged by changing sex role expectations culturally, and astonished at the obstinacy of my own habits of mind; frustrated by my ineptitude in some parent-child interactions, and awestruck at the graceful forces which swept in to redeem others.
>
> My hunch is that such stirrings of feeling, and the responses one makes to them, constitute most of what matters about human life. All the rest—all the going and coming, getting and spending, building and breaking and building again—are probably the lesser part, even though they apparently dominate our days.
>
> Eliot A. Daley, *Father Feelings: A Loving Account of the Trials and Joys of Being a Father*

Nurture is a human practice that fosters the growth and development of individuals and institutions. It has been assumed that women are better at nurturing children than men. As a result, nurturing is one of those human practices underdeveloped in men. There is, however, nothing in the definition of the word "nurture" that excludes men. When we say that someone is a nurturing person or when we describe an environment as nurturing, we mean to suggest that both the person and the context promote growth toward maturation. When nurture is a verb about raising children, it implies cherishing those we nurture. We also distinguish between nurture and nature to emphasize the elements of environment that influence the development of a self in contrast to genes and chromosomes as heredity factors that also shape who we become.

Not all men are nurturing all the time. The persistence of child abuse by men is explored in chapter three. The emphasis on nurture introduces the need for an environment that is safe enough for growth to occur. Children need fathers, other men, and environments that will nurture and protect them. The National Association for the Prevention of Child Abuse and Neglect of Australia prepared a declaration for men on the protection of children that I have modified into the following statement:

> I will not physically harm a child.
> I will not humiliate or intimidate a child privately
>   or in public.
> I will not use a child sexually
> . . . and I will speak out against those who do.
> *I will teach my son to respect women and children.*
> *I will publicly declare in word and deed the importance*
>   *of fathering.*
> *I will work to create a world in which men are the*
>   *nurturers that all*
> *children deserve.*
> I will urge that the sexualization and exploitation of children
> by business and
> media industries be confronted and stopped.
> *I will speak out against attitudes and actions that demean*
>   *children and*
> *vigorously challenge local Christian congregations to become*
> *sanctuaries for childhood committed to the well-being of*
>   *all children.*[5]

So much has been written, spoken, and visualized about the abuse of children by men that it should not have to be said again here. The reference to an Australian association against child abuse by men is a painful illustration that this tragic issue is not limited to the United States. Despite men's best intentions, this does not seem to be a problem that will go away. If, however, every man who reads this book would share this pledge with family and friends and promise to speak publicly about his commitment to abide by this pledge, we would take one small step toward altering the abusive behavior of fathers and men against children. I make that promise to the reader.

NURTURING MOMENTS FOR MEN AT THE BEGINNING OF LIFE

One aspect of the gender revolution is that mothers are no longer the only ones who have "children on their minds" all day long. Fathers who share fully in the nurture of their children will need to know that Thursday is cello lessons, swim practice starts early on Wednesday and Friday, and a child's dental appointment is Monday afternoon. If fathers and mothers share the nurturing responsibilities, the full-time work of parenting may be shared. Even if they cannot be present physically, fathers can be mindful of their children. Thinking about, talking about, worrying about, praying for our children, however, never ends even if it is shared. That is another way of paying attention.

At the beginning of life, paying attention is a primal, bodily relationship. Holding an infant, smiling at this astounding gift of life is itself nurturing and creates an environment for nurture. It is often observed that fathers have difficulty overcoming the initial bond between the mother and infant that begins during pregnancy. Sometimes fathers feel like outsiders in the process of pregnancy, delivery, and nursing. While there is no desire to diminish the special bond children and mothers have, fathers need to do what they can to deepen in themselves an awareness of the birth of a child. The following poem conveys the anguish of a father when that bond cannot be made at the beginning.

> Then did she tell you
> Where I was
> On the night of the storm,
> Of the rain,
> Of the restaurant;
> Some friend
> Who had seen her
> Said, "When are you
> Having that baby of yours?"
> And your mother said
> "Now," and she did.

You can only remember
Because she had told you
When maybe you asked.
Or maybe she saw you,
In the sun, turning restless,
And she told you a story
Of the night you were born.

But did she tell you
The weekend we went
To Nantucket
And the sun, and her laughter
When I ran on the shore
With Canadian Geese.
I caught one and cradled
Its soft curve of white feathers.

I don't remember
Because I wasn't there
And I didn't see you
On the night of the storm
Of the rain,
Of your birth.
I don't think I told you.[6]

I am haunted by the pathos in this poem of a father's absence. Whatever the reason, it reflects the unspoken and maybe even unacknowledged anguish of fathers who did not see their children on the night of their birth. In addition to being present at the birth, there are a number of things that fathers can do to deepen the bond with our children from the beginning.

- It may begin simply by telling people at work or play that your wife is pregnant.
- Hearing the heartbeat or seeing a picture of new life forming helps to make the process more concrete for fathers.
- When fathers take more responsibility preparing the baby's room, they are doing what they can to make a safe environment for the baby. My son-in-law, Gilbert, painted a mural on a wall and the ceiling of Julia's room as his way of preparing for her coming.

- One young father I know slept on the baby's first blanket so that the smell of the father's body would be close to the newborn even when the father could not be.

- If the sex of the unborn is known, it makes it easier to address the yet unborn life in a personal way. As a grandfather two thousand miles away from where my grandson, Jonah, was born, it made a difference that I could greet Jonah by name fully five months before he was born.

- The presence of men and women together in birthing classes has contributed greatly to diminishing the feeling men have had that they are incidental to the process. My son and daughter-in-law still meet with a group of couples who went through Lamaze together. It has become a remarkable support group for both fathers and mothers that continues to gather around the birthdays of the children and the birth of new children.

- When my son was born, it was still not possible for me as a father to be present in the room. Thankfully that rule has changed and fathers are welcome in the birthing room and may even have important work to do coaching the mother with her breathing.

- In the first months of a child's life, there are a host of little things that fathers can do like feeding the baby through the night, cleaning bottles, making formula, and changing diapers. What is most important is that men no longer think about those activities as helping mothers with *their* work but as sharing in the common nurturing responsibilities fathers and mothers have together.

A former student once described his first meetings with his sons. He was able to hold his first son shortly after the birth and walk "up and down drab hallways for three hours. I held him as close to my face as I could lift him, and told him how wonderful it was finally to see him. The second son's birth was more problematic. Both he and his mother nearly died. I rocked him in a hard wooden chair. I told him how special he was to me because soon after he was conceived, I had become seriously ill and had almost died. I looked at him and held him with a tenderness and love I could not have imagined before that moment."

Not every new father can speak so directly to a newborn infant or even hold such a fragile creature. We can, however, see our children as whole persons, unique and full of mystery. From the beginning, we bond with our children by paying attention.

RAISING A CHILD

In *Fatherless America*, David Blankenhorn paints a bleak picture of deadbeat dads, absentee fathers, and children who suffer. He contends that men are not suited for responsible fatherhood. Rather, they are inclined to sexual promiscuity and paternal waywardness. Blankenhorn concludes that because men do not volunteer for fatherhood, they must be conscripted into it by an "authoritative story about fatherhood" from the culture. "Cultures must . . . devise and enforce the father role for men, coaxing and guiding them into fatherhood through a set of legal and extralegal pressures that require them to maintain a close alliance with their children's mother and to invest in their children."7 Men do not generally respond positively to being forced or even coerced into particular behavior. Even coaxing does not always work.

For Christian fathers, the Scriptures and general teachings of the church provide an authoritative story about fatherhood that compels us to keep exploring new ways to fulfill our responsibility. The biblical story is neither about coercion or conscription. It does insist, however, that there is nothing greater than a child and that we are not to hinder children in any way. Beyond requiring a safe and cherishing environment, nurturing our children includes recognition of their unique gifts, clarity about our values, a commitment to provide the physical and emotional nourishment necessary for growth, and attention to the rhythms of human biology across the life cycle and the sacred rhythms of life.

Physical absence is one dilemma. However, fathers may be in a family but still be absent. My own father was more a pastor than a father until the later years of his life. I was determined not be like my father, but I still followed his pattern when my children were young. Some men are emotionally absent because they are preoccupied with work or other matters. Others have to work long hours at low wages in order to support their family. We may even distort reality enough to believe that a superficial connection is sufficient.

The lyrics to *Cat's in the Cradle*, written by Sandy and Harry Chapin, document how men are trapped in patterns they learned from their fathers and unwillingly pass on to their sons.

> My child arrived just the other day.
> He came to the world in the usual way.
> But there were planes to catch and bills to pay.
> He learned to walk while I was away.
> And he was talkin' 'fore I knew it, and as he grew

He'd say, "I'm gonna be like you, dad,
You know I'm gonna be like you.

My son turned ten just the other day.
He said, "Thanks for the ball, dad, come on let's play.
Can you teach me to throw?" I said, "Not today
I got a lot to do." He said, "That's O.K."
And he walked away, but his smile never dimmed,
And said, "I'm gonna be like him, yeah,
You know I'm gonna be like.

Well he came home from college just the other day
So much like a man I just had to say
"Son, I'm proud of you can you sit down for a while?"
He shook his head and said with a smile,
"What I'd really like is to borrow the car keys.
See you later. Can I have them please?"

I've long since retired. My son's moved away.
I called him up just the other day.
I said I'd like to see you if you don't mind."
He said, "I'd love to see you dad if I can find the time.
You see my new job's a hassle and the kids have the flu
But it's sure nice talking to you, dad,
It's been sure nice talking to you."
And as I hung up the phone it occurred to me—
He'd grown up just like me.
My boy was just like me.[8]

The song tells the story of too many fathers and sons. It is a story of missed opportunities to nurture our children. It is a painful picture of superficiality that covers emptiness. The chorus to the song includes a line that is repeated after each stanza: "We'll get together then. You know we'll have a good time then." The song poignantly illustrates how easy it is for sons to imitate their fathers.

If fathers determine to be present in the family, how shall they act or what shall they do? There is not enough space in this chapter to explore the skills of being a nurturing parent. All the themes of this book, however, contribute to understanding how to be a good husband and father. *If a man sees the uniqueness of each child, shares feelings more easily, manages aggression, shares power with his children as well as his wife, practices vulnerability, learns how to make and keep friends, handles disappointment, and grieves openly, he will be a good father.* There are skills about disciplining and resolving conflict that may need to be learned but they will only work if they flow from the character of a man who has sought to develop his full humanity as a sign of faithfulness.

BLESSING AND LETTING GO

The story of Jacob begins and ends with blessing. We would not be faithful to the presence of Jacob's story in our stories if we did not explore the significance of blessing. Blessing is an act of recognition. A blessing may not say, "I approve," but it always says, "I recognize." It acknowledges the uniqueness of an individual. Jacob's deception was a theft of Esau's unique identity as the first one out of the womb. A blessing is a promise thrown into the future. Yahweh's promise to Abraham that he would father a great nation is continued with Jacob because of and despite his chicanery. Moral purity is not a condition for the promise and so Jacob is in the line through which God's promise continues. "Know that I am with you and will keep you wherever you go, and will bring you back to this land; for I will not leave you until I have done what I have promised you" (Gen. 28:15). It is the blessing of God that sustains all life. The blessing that parents give is a mutual recognition of God's promise to accompany our children into an uncertain future.[9]

With God, blessings are unlimited. For human folk, and perhaps for men in particular, blessings are limited. In anguish, Esau presses his father to give him a blessing too but Jacob received the only one Isaac could give. Sometimes it is that way with fathers. We bless one child but not the others—not so much because they are undeserving but because many fathers do not have much to give away. One other impediment to blessing a child as a father is that many were not themselves blessed. In the world of expressing feelings, it is difficult to give what has not been given. Fathers who are reluctant to bless their children may not know what it is or what it means because they have not received a blessing. For myself, the absence of blessing has been like a hole in the soul that established the presence of emotional poverty where promise should reside.

Blessing our children changes their status. The promise of leaving home and letting go is often closely linked to the bestowing of a blessing. It is one of the ways that we make friends with our adult children. True, sons and daughters are forever sons and daughters but they are no longer children. The recognition of this changed status frees children struggling to define their adult status to stay close to home without fear that they will be forced to return to child status. A blessing is the confirmation of emotional separateness that makes being friends possible. "When parents and their adult children are friends they share all the present and future concerns that other friends share, along with their shared biography."[10] Like all good friendships, fathers and sons can promise to walk together in freedom into an unknown future sustained by God's presence. As most fathers know, making friends with your children is one of the surprising gifts of parenting.

SHARING FAITH

We cannot live with authenticity or integrity without knowing what we believe. If men and fathers (and women and mothers) do not know clearly what they believe, it is not surprising that our children do not know either. Our children often know who is our favorite baseball player or hockey team or our opinion of a political figure before they know what we believe about God. Because being the spiritual head of a family is no longer an entitlement for most men, our own formation in faith becomes an even more critical dimension of preparing for our role in fatherly nurture.

A man of integrity is someone who is willing to say publicly that he is acting in accord with what he believes. That is a risky thing to do because it means our lives can be measured by standards of coherence between what we say and what we do. A father who cheats on income tax or constantly interrupts when others are speaking will and should have difficulty enforcing rules about not interrupting at the dinner table or cheating on a school test. Our children need to see a genuine connection in us between what we say and what we do, between what we disclose of our inner world and the outer self that can be seen. Children watch what we do more than they listen to what we say. Sharing faith in that context requires that we seek coherence between what we say and how we act.

After his young adult son, Kieran, had called to tell his father about organizing a successful work stoppage in the north of Australia, his father, Doug Purnell, whose art appears throughout this book, wrote these words as a father and a friend to his son. They embody the kind of authenticity that makes faithful nurturing and nurturing for faithfulness possible.

> I am proud of your ability to achieve these things, always working for the greater social good. Your brother told me that you had a hard time after the work stoppage with a friend in banking management. The conversation upset you so much that you walked away from dinner. I think I was 27 when I went through some hard times because

my emotions overflowed and I did not know what to do with them. Your job is a tough one. It will, at times, be quite lonely. There will be more difficult times. You will need to know who you are and have a source of inner strength to stand firm in hard places. That is what social and prophetic leadership is about.

My conversations with Brian Howe have taught me how important it is to have an undergirding philosophy that nourishes me as a person and helps me fashion a social vision. I am a Christian person not because I am interested in heaven or need to be saved. I am a Christian because it is the guiding story that calls me forward and nourishes my life and challenges me to work for the social good. Love and Peace, Dad

Doug's transparency to his son became the occasion not only to reveal himself but give a blessing to his son. Faithfulness in nurturing our children is formed out of being authentic rather than living falsely. Although men may have mastered the art of deception in the public arena in order to present a competent persona, it is more difficult, and actually not necessary, to hide in the home. Our children already know when their fathers are faking, hiding, or being inauthentic. This realization should be reason enough to compel men to seek out and participate in communities of faith in order to get the support they need to embody a new vision of being a man. In order to embody this new vision of manhood, men will need to practice being vulnerable in the church in order to be more authentic at home. Authenticity is the gift fathers can give their children that comes from practicing their Christian faith.

MAKING AND KEEPING FRIENDS

There is no direct reference to friendship in the biblical story of Jacob. That is not unusual because the family was the primary context for intimacy in the ancient Near East. Relationships outside the family were largely political and economic. Those connections still required trust and mutuality. The Hebrew word for friend may also mean "another person" or "neighbor." Because the Jacob story is about continuing God's promise to Abraham to fashion a nation out of one family, the primary focus is that family story. It is also about a family surviving, and even thriving, in an alien land. Because the webs of human connectedness were primarily within the bonds of family, living as a stranger on foreign soil was never easy. When there was a famine in Canaan, the land God had promised to Abraham and his descendants, Isaac was forced to leave his kinfolk to survive as an alien among the Philistines. "Reside in this land as an alien," the Lord said to Isaac, "and I will be with you, and will bless you" (Gen. 26:3). In all the stories about living among strangers, God was a constant friend and companion to Abraham, Isaac, and Jacob.

There were, however, tensions with the neighbors. Isaac, the immigrant, became rich in the land that did not belong to him. In order to establish peace, Isaac made a covenant with his neighbors in which they promised to do no harm to one another. Being such a neighbor is one kind of friendship. Unfortunately, that covenant was violated in the next generation when Jacob's daughter Dinah was raped by Shechem and again when Simeon and Levi, sons of Jacob, deceived Hamor and Shechem by killing all the males in the city to avenge the rape of their sister (see Genesis 34). Living as neighbors in the midst of strangers, like making and keeping friends, begins with trust and mutual respect. When trust is broken and covenants are violated, friendships are threatened.

Centuries after Jacob, in a social context in which kinship networks are more limited and the public world is increasingly impersonal, men still struggle with making and keeping friends. Men will have fishing or hunting buddies, golf or poker partners. They have work-related acquaintances with whom important bonds exist that may also serve a business purpose or fit their work schedule. Men will help a neighbor fix a toilet or build a barbecue for the neighborhood picnic, but they may not share with that same neighbor a diagnosis of prostate cancer or the pain of losing a job. When men are asked if they have a best friend, many will insist it is their wife. Being and having friends is an underdeveloped practice for most men, even though they may admit to being lonely and looking for friendship. From an early age, men learn to compete but not relate. Men are reluctant to acknowledge they have emotional needs that others could fill because that might give their competition an unfair advantage.

Making and keeping friends has been a personal issue for me. For a long time in my life I did not do well with friendship. I had good colleagues at work, I had parishioners or students for whom I was an authority, I had people in my life who were my superiors, I had a wife and children, but I had few friends. About twenty-five years ago, around the time I turned forty, I made a decision to focus on friendship. Now I cannot imagine surviving without the friendships of men and women. They are a constant source of support and challenge. They are people with whom I can brag without being embarrassed. Because they know me well, I cannot discount their love. It endures. I have been particularly blessed by having friends who will say things to me I do not want to hear.

THE GIFT OF FRIENDSHIP

Friendship is a gift and a sign. It is a gift that invites God and all those whom God loves into deep and enduring relationships. It is a sign that human beings are creatures whose goodness requires belonging and a sense of community. In that sense, friendship is central to the moral life. It is also necessary for survival. We cannot endure without friendships of one kind or another. That is what I understand Martin Marty to mean when he writes that "we have friends or we are friends in order that we do not get killed."[1] Friendship is like breathing: living depends on it. I am a friend of others when their needs evoke a spontaneous willingness to respond for the sake of their well-being. My neediness invokes the same response from a friend.

Friendship is more than just survival. The radical vision of God's reign that we see in the life and ministry of Jesus is directed toward the outcaste and the stranger. According to that vision, it is not a particularly Christian virtue to invite our friends to dinner. Jesus intends that we break down the old walls of exclusiveness that separate people and establish a new community in Christ beyond reciprocity—beyond loving those who love us back. Christians are admonished to love as God loves without expecting anything in return. It is not surprising that friendship is regularly overlooked because it depends on mutuality. Nonetheless, the community formed by Christ is a fellowship of belonging governed by a spirit of mutuality.

Jesus established friendship as a model for Christian living with these words to his disciples: "You are my friends if you do what I command you. I do not call you servants any longer, because the servant does not know what the master is doing; but I have called you friends, because I have made known to you everything that I have heard from my Father" (John 15:14–15). Full disclosure, Jesus implies, is one mark of being friends. Hierarchical relationships, in which we are not given the information we need to respond appropriately or act responsibly, are not based on friendship and are alien to Christian discipleship. In order to be sustained in Christian faithfulness, men need to foster communities of friends that will support them in loving those who do not love in return.

SOLITARY MEN AND THE NEED FOR FRIENDSHIP

Pictures of solitary men leading the charge against an enemy, braving the elements to conquer new territory, sitting alone on a tractor, or moving a corporation to new levels of excellence and power dominate the stories we tell about male heroes in the culture and in our families.

Not knowing how to make and keep friends is one consequence of promoting that solitary behavior in men. However, the "lonesome cowboy" is an isolating image that results in loneliness and the inability to foster the kind of relational skills and mutuality of spirit that friendship requires. New patterns of leadership have challenged the assumption that loneliness is the necessary price of success or effective leadership. Being and having friends does not contradict the strength of solitude. Rather, fostering friendship expands our understanding of being human and strengthens the awareness that being human is always communal. Human dimensions like being vulnerable, nurturing, and expressing feelings explored elsewhere in this book depend on this communal sense that we learn from friendship.

Many years ago, a man I knew lost his wife. Keith's wife died suddenly and tragically after falling down the stairs in their home. He was understandably devastated and withdrew from the people they knew together. Eventually Keith came back to the church choir and later reconnected with the theatre group that had been a significant part of Julie's life, but his eyes were empty. About a year after Julie's tragic and untimely death, his pastor invited him to write about his needs. He identified fourteen needs. The last one was on friendship.

> I need a friend. I am not a good friend to have right now unless someone will stick with the friendship for a long time. I hide for such a long time. I am close to only a few people and only one lives nearby. I talk to him a lot but I am afraid he is getting tired of me. Because I am so lonely, I feel that I must make myself available to some individuals who could be my friends.

Many men will identify with Keith's struggle. We need friends but we have had such a long history of hiding brokenness or evading pain that we don't know if we could ever be a friend. Keith was needy but he did not understand that being a friend requires a willingness to risk being needy. One aim for men is to overcome the fear of neediness and helplessness in order to stretch out our hands to others in friendship and respond to others when they reach out to us. There are, however, many other obstacles to friendship between men that are so much a part of our life context that we are often unaware of their presence.

IMPEDIMENTS TO FRIENDSHIP

Even if men could overcome their resistance to neediness and mutual vulnerability, there are social forces that impede friendship. *First, needing a friend challenges cultural expectations of self-sufficiency and independence.* When a spirit of radical individualism and independence in men is coupled with competitive consumerism, shared activities are no longer occasions for relating but battlegrounds for winning and losing. People formed by a consumerist society are often deficient in the deeper spiritual resources necessary for friendship, particularly justice, generosity, compassion, availability, and true freedom of spirit. If we believe that what we possess is more important than whom we love, we will spend more time making money than making friends. If we are also keeping score—even in our heads—then men will spend more time keeping up the lawn than keeping up friendships.

The second impediment from the culture might be described by the phrase *the way we live.* That is, the way we live diminishes the possibility of friendships happening out of common interaction of men through activities at work, church, or play. The phenomenon of fragmentation and isolation in society has been captured by Robert Putnam's book *Bowling Alone.*[2] If his analysis of American individualism is accurate, it will certainly be more difficult to make friends as more people bowl alone instead of in teams or groups. Because men are more likely to begin (and sustain) friendships with shared activity, the decrease in public social activities is problematic: it diminishes opportunities for friendship making. Furthermore, the fast pace of modern societies makes friendship more difficult by limiting the time available to build enduring bonds. Internet chat rooms and long-distance e-mail correspondence may take the edge off loneliness but they cannot substitute for a friend's hug.

When it is assumed that all (or most) emotional needs *should* be satisfied in the family, having friends who are not in the family may be discouraged and even be regarded as an act of disloyalty, which is the third impediment. In that sense, *the primacy of family* limits who might be a friend or how much time is available for friends. I remember a situation that my son faced when he was in high school. He had a friend with whom he shared a great deal. But the friendship ended because my son's friend frequently canceled their plans together whenever his family decided to do something together. For people whose daily social network is the extended family, it is possible to have all or most of one's emotional needs met within the family. When husbands report that their wives are their best friends, they are promoting a similar view of *the primacy of family* as the context for friendship.

Lover is one of the four images of being a man that Robert Moore and Douglas Gillette identified in their book *King, Warrior, Magician, Lover.* Their aim was to help men access the positive potentials within us that ancient mythologies have linked with these images. It is the lover energy, they suggest, that helps men "feel related, connected, alive, enthusiastic, compassionate, empathic, energized, and romantic about our lives, our goals, our work, and our achievements."³ To be a lover is a wonderful image for intimacy and belonging. There is also an element of power attached to being a lover because it implies the capacity to seduce. The promotion of genital sex in popular culture supports *lover* as the primary metaphor for male intimacy. Men will always be lovers, that is certain. But when being a lover is more about dominance or power over another person than mutuality, *being a lover impedes friendship*. This impediment to friendship in a man is revealed when he loses interest in being a lover if a wife or woman partner becomes more autonomous. In order to practice being a friend, men need to discover ways to be intimate that are marked by equality and mutuality.

> A friend is one to whom one may pour out all the contents of one's heart, chaff and grain together, knowing that the gentlest hands will take and sift it, keep what is worth keeping and with a breath of kindness blow the rest away.
>
> *Arabian proverb*

In many Christian traditions, the normative understanding of love is *agape*—God's way of loving that is not self-seeking and does not depend on mutuality. Christians are encouraged to love the way God loves even though it is highly unlikely that we can achieve that level of loving. A second form of love, *eros* or erotic love, is an inescapable dimension of being human that we are often taught to hold in check. The third biblical word for love, *philia* or friendship, has been overlooked by most Christian traditions. As a result, friendship has not been promoted in churches as one expression of Christian life.

Friendship is a gift from God for the meantime. As an unknown fourteenth-century monk once observed: "Holy friendship truly is from God, that amid the wretchedness of this exile, we be comforted with the counsel of friends until we come to him." Friendships will not save us, but they are still a gift from God who chooses to give us daily bread, good weather, good times, and good friends. To love as God loves certainly is the Christian ideal. That is what we aim for. And it is more than friendship. In the meantime, however, we need friends until we come to rest in God.

LONELINESS, SOLITUDE, AND FRIENDSHIP

Men may say they left a party because it was boring, there was nothing to do, they didn't know anybody or nobody talked to them, and that may be true. What they experienced could also have been the anguish of loneliness even though they would not call it that. Loneliness is the pain of disconnectedness often hidden behind male bravado or busyness or indifference. It is an experience of deprivation, of being without people who love us and fill us up. Loneliness is aching to be touched, longing to be heard, but afraid no one will listen or understand. It is a feeling of not belonging even when we do. Cellular phones make constant connections possible but do not eliminate the deeper loneliness that is part of the human condition. *Loneliness occurs when our ordinary and necessary needs for attachment and affection are not met.*

We experience loneliness when our world is smaller or less satisfying than we had hoped it would be. We experience loneliness when the company sends us to an unfamiliar place, when the college dorm is filled with people whose interests or values we don't share, when we are hospitalized or confined to home and nobody calls, or when we have a hearing loss that isolates us during social conversation. We experience loneliness when someone we love dies. Loneliness comes with loving. In that sense, it is an unavoidable and even necessary gift because in the darkness of loneliness, men discover their longing for connection and the deeper desire to love and be loved. Because it takes courage to examine loneliness, it is often a silent and unacknowledged companion in men's lives.

I was once in a support group of men that was made up of friends and colleagues active and successful in teaching pastoral care or the practice of pastoral counseling. All of us were happily married, gainfully employed, connected to our young adult children, financially secure, respected by our peers, and *lonely*. One remarkable afternoon all six of us talked for three hours about the levels of loneliness in our lives. It is probably true that our high expectations of emotional and intellectual intimacy increased the likelihood that we would experience loneliness. And yet, like many men, we were often frozen between wanting the intimacy of friendship and running from it. Unfortunately, the group unraveled when one member went through loneliness and grief that was hidden from the rest of us.

Loneliness is born in fear and suspicion that no one loves us without strings attached, that no place is safe from manipulation or abuse. If our experience of the world leads to mistrust and skepticism, it is unlikely we will be able to trust people enough with our story to diminish loneliness. Fear of violence, prompting people to barricade themselves behind doubled-bolted doors or security gates, intensifies loneliness in cities. Church historian Martin Marty once observed that we can "kill people with a gun and we can kill them with an apartment."4 If we regard the world as a dangerous place, we may conclude that loneliness is simply the discomforting consequence of modern living. More men live alone, bowl alone, travel alone, eat alone. Not every man who lives alone is lonely but men who live alone are prone to loneliness.

> [Friendship] requires that another man know you, but also that he know himself enough to stop the macho posturing and competing. When you know a man, when you come to realize that by knowing yourself you know all men, you don't need the envy anymore. You can join the company of men and begin mutual emulation. . . . I feel most heroic, and most intimately a member of the fraternity of men, when I am exposing and exploring with other men what we have learned, what we all know but have been trained not to say, about the common journey of manhood.
>
> Frank Pittman, *Man Enough: Fathers, Sons, and the Search for Masculinity*

For much of my early life, I equated being alone with loneliness. When I was ten years old, our front porch was the neighborhood social center. Then we moved to a village with less than one hundred people. It had no neighborhood and few children my own age. Sunday afternoon walks with my dog were a regular experience of loneliness through my adolescence. In recent years, however, I have learned to be more comfortable with solitude. Solitude is a way of being alone without loneliness. The movement from loneliness to solitude is a journey of the heart from sadness and despair to deep inner peace. The aim of solitude is to be sufficient for one's self and hence not dependent on others to eliminate our boredom or overcome our melancholy. When we can be alone without being lonely, we are more likely to make and keep friends because the capacity for solitude preserves the freedom necessary for friendship. We are often drawn to people or seek their friendship for reasons that remain a mystery to us. But what keeps a friendship going is not a mystery: it is intentional commitment, hard work, staying in touch, shared interests, honoring freedom, and the willingness to risk mutual vulnerability.

CHARACTERISTICS OF FRIENDSHIP

Authentic friendship is characterized by freedom, shared interests, mutuality, and trust.

Freedom

We cannot be coerced to be a friend. Nor can we force someone to be our friend. We do not create friendship by manipulating from a position of need. Friendship is a voluntary relationship freely chosen. The following words, written by Dietrich Bonhoeffer from a prison cell during World War II, express the centrality of freedom for friendship.

> Not from the heavy soil,
> where blood and sex and oath
> rule in their hallowed might,
> where earth itself,
> guarding the primal consecrated order,
> avenges wantonness and madness—
> . . . but from the spirit's choice and free desire,
> needing no oath or legal bond,
> is friend bestowed on friend.[5]

Most relationships are ringed with duty, utility, or desire. Friendship, however, is formed in "the spirit's free choice." Although establishing a friendship is a voluntary activity, it is not necessarily self-conscious. Sooner or later, however, we need to decide mutually and intentionally that we *are* friends and would like to remain so.

Shared Interests

Friendships often begin with an experience of common interest or activities. Hunting, playing golf, playing cards, fishing together, having small children at the same time, watching the same sport, belonging to the same church, sharing a common political point of view, and surviving the same illness are activities, interests, and shared experiences that bond people to one another. Organizations in the church and community often provide the occasion for people to meet around a common vision. My wife and I are constantly amazed by the depth of connection we have with people we knew thirty years ago when our children were young. We were all poor, struggling, and willing to be vulnerable with one another. We needed one another in ways that have been more difficult to acknowledge as we have grown older and more established. However important shared activities or common interests might be, friendship will need to go deeper to endure. Discovering the places of "shared mindfulness" is part of this process.

Mutuality

Near the beginning of a novel based on the imagined life of a twelfth-century English hermit saint, Godric, Frederick Buechner makes this observation about the friendship between Godric and Mouse.

> Nonetheless our fights were few those first, far days. We loved each other, Mouse and I, and our love was born of need, for so it always is with mortal folk. God's love's all gift, for God has need of naught, but human folk love one another for the way they fill each other's emptiness. I needed Mouse for his strength and mirth and daring. Mouse needed me for my mettle and my wit.[6]

A friend is our needs met. In a friendship that endures there is a recognition of mutual dependency. One of the reasons why it is difficult for men to be and have friends is that it challenges the myth of male self-sufficiency. Someone recently diagnosed with prostate cancer admitted this: *"My own self-sufficiency has hurt me for I have very few friends."* We are inclined to think if we can't do it ourselves, it can't be done. Sometimes men would rather fail miserably than admit we cannot do it all by ourselves.

> Friendships are not sought, they emerge. They take shape among people of shared purpose, they grow from the soil of similar interests and concerns. . . . Friendship is not just a good for the moral life, it is indispensable; there simply is no other way to come in touch with the goods that make us whole than through relationships with those who share them. That is why we can say friendship is the crucible of moral development, the center of moral formation.
>
> Paul J. Wadell, *Friendship and the Moral Life*

At least for me, being and having friends is quite simply a matter of survival. I am quite clear that I cannot make it as a man today without a company of friends who will *hear my story* (probably several times), *tell me the truth about myself* (even when I say I don't want to hear it), *protect me from myself* (especially when I want to do something foolish), *hold me when I am afraid* (which may include keeping me from running away), *and celebrate with me when I succeed.* I am a friend for others when their needs evoke in me a spontaneous willingness to respond for the sake of their well-being. At this deep level of human need, being and having friends requires the willingness to risk.

Trust

The willingness to risk depends on trust. We are willing to be vulnerable only in the company of those we trust. When the delicate balance of reciprocal vulnerability is not maintained, friendship is diminished. The men's gathering in which I participated disintegrated because one man chose not to share the pain he was experiencing as his wife was dying. It was certainly his choice to keep that pain private but it did have consequences for our mutual trust. When I have held back my struggles from a friend, when my friend's response does not match my need, or when my friend has gone through a difficult patch in his life that I later find out about, trust is diminished by the unwillingness to risk. We do not hide our needs from friends. Men who have difficulty being vulnerable to another will have friendships of limited depth. Friendship for men is too often like racquetball with rules and a scoreboard in one's head. Fear, loneliness, and isolation are diminished when our hearts are filled with love, but our hearts can be filled only when our hands can receive. Open hands to receive, trusting what the friend will give, is a sign of the willingness to risk for the sake of friendship.

INITIATIVES THAT ENHANCE FRIENDSHIP

Being a friend is a part of being human. It is also an essential characteristic of Christian faithfulness. For many men, developing the art of friendship requires acting intentionally to challenge old male practices. Here are some intentional actions I have found helpful in nurturing that change.

Call a friend for no reason whatsoever. Men in particular need to practice calling without an agenda, just to be in touch. The message we send is that the friendship has value in itself. If just calling for no reason is too risky, tell someone you would like to have as a friend how much you appreciated something they did some time ago. Compliments are not dangerous. Or find out his birthday and send one of those silly cards that mocks men.

Be the first to self-disclose. Honest vulnerability begets more honesty.

And when it does not, we discover the limits of a relationship early. If we wait for the other person to be self-revealing, we may never discover the freedom of being vulnerable. The willingness to be vulnerable with a friend will sustain us through lonely times and keep us safe until we come to God. If we practice honest vulnerability, we need to be prepared to be disappointed when it is not reciprocated.

Don't make pain the price of a beer. As a freshman in college I had two roommates who were regularly able to needle me to tears. When I told them how much the humiliation hurt, they laughed and said they mocked me because they loved me. If you ask the question, "Why do I put myself through this?" every time you talk to someone, then *your* pain may be *his* reason for keeping the friendship alive. On the other hand, if a friend is both interesting and complex, we may have to swallow some guff to keep it going.

Call a friend facing a big decision. Friendships are built by the communication of affection and admiration and by the willingness to take initiative to honor time together. A call recognizing that a friend is facing a big decision or a time of stress at work is a gift of affection that builds trust.

Talk about changes in the friendship. Because people change, friendships will change. It is important to recognize life changes and renegotiate the terms of a friendship rather than fight to hold on to outmoded patterns.

Talk about friendship. It may take a while to reach this point but it is important. Or it may be the place you begin to establish a bond with someone whom you discover shares your longing for friendship. If for no other reason, talking about friendship is an important step because men would rather leave difficult things unsaid. In a society that tends to regard relationships as expendable and friendships as replaceable, men need to go against the tide by declaring the value of this special friendship.

Don't cross the imaginary line. In a way, that maxim is the opposite of the invitation to talk about changes and the friendship. We know when there are things that cannot be talked about. Salaries are one. Having an affair may be another. If an evening together with a friend ends abruptly or with a lame excuse, you may have crossed the imaginary line of privacy. With good friends, the transgression does not strike a mortal blow. The dilemma, however, is that men do not talk with other men about the kind of pain that is simply too hard for us to bear alone or in the company of others.

Find friendship in God. When the psalmist says, "My soul thirsts for

God, for the living God," he points to a deep emptiness and loneliness in human life that only God can fill. If we live in God, then we are more likely to transform loneliness to solitude on the way to friendship. If we live in God and endure loneliness, then our friendships will be born in neediness and freedom.

THE CHURCH AS A COMMUNITY OF FRIENDS

There are many places in society to make friends and sustain friendships. The local congregation has the potential to be such a place for men seeking friendship. At the moment, it is more potential than actual. It is an awkward time for women and men in the church. My experience at the 2001 General Assembly of the Presbyterian Church (U.S.A.) is a parable of our present dilemma. I had gone to the Assembly to speak to a luncheon for men about this book. Prior to lunch, I wandered about the display area looking for the Men's Ministries booth. None of the men I asked seemed to know what it was or where it was. A few were vaguely aware of its presence. Finally, a couple of women took pity on my plight and suggested I go to the women's booth/area. "They will know where the men are." Shortly after, quite by accident, I found the half table that was representing Men's Ministries to the Assembly.

This story is repeated in many denominations. Women's programs will have bigger budgets, longer display tables, and a larger staff than parallel programs for men. As long as women perceive the church to be patriarchal and male, they will see little need for a special program area for men. Men, on the hand, feel dispossessed and alienated from a church they once dominated. The reality is that men may still outnumber women in church leadership but women are in the pews. Unless national church bodies of Christian denominations seek to rectify this imbalance, independent organizations like Promise Keepers will appeal to men who are looking for a place to fashion a new vision of manhood. When men's programs are initiated, it is crucial that they reflect at least some of the concerns of this book. Men do not need projects to draw them together and to the church. They need time and freedom and a modicum of respect and safety to explore together in the company of friends the complexities of being a modern man of faith.

LEARNING TO GRIEVE

Loss is at the center of Jacob's story. He lost his homeland when he cheated Esau out of the blessing. Jacob lost his innocence when Laban trapped him in fourteen years of servitude in order to have Rachel, whom he loved, as his wife. Then there was the limp and a name change, both of which profoundly altered Jacob's approach to the world. While the change was a good thing, it was nonetheless a loss. Jacob's response is more one of gratitude: "I have seen God face to face, and yet my life is preserved" (Gen. 32:30).

Two significant deaths in the life of Jacob are described quite matter-of-factly in ten consecutive verses of Genesis 35. Rachel died in childbirth. As she was dying, "she named [her son] Ben-oni [son of my suffering]; but his father [Jacob] called him Benjamin [son of the right hand]" (Gen. 35:18). (One can only imagine and hope that Jacob ignored his dying wife's wish because he did not want to be reminded of Rachel's suffering whenever he called his youngest son.) "So Rachel died, . . . and Jacob set up a pillar at her grave; it is the pillar of Rachel's tomb, which is there to this day. Israel [Jacob] journeyed on, and pitched his tent beyond the tower of Eder" (Gen. 35:18–21). (No weeping, no lament, no cancelled trip. Just a grave marker.) When his father, Isaac, died, Jacob was present with him and "his sons Esau and Jacob buried him" (Gen. 35:29). Between these two deaths, Jacob was humiliated by his son Reuben, who had intercourse with Jacob's concubine, Bilhah. (Again, no rage, no lament.)

The one moment of loss in the life of Jacob for which he did grieve intensely was temporary, though he did not know it at the time. Jacob's sons had sold their brother Joseph to traders who took him to Egypt. The brothers then slaughtered a goat, dipped Joseph's special cloak in the goat's blood, and presented the bloody cloak to Jacob as evidence of the death of his favored son. "Then Jacob tore his garments, and put sackcloth on his loins, and mourned for his son many days. All his sons and all his daughters sought to comfort him; but he refused to be comforted, and said, 'No, I shall go down to Sheol to my son, mourning.' Thus his father bewailed him" (Gen. 37:34–35). Although Jacob's life had been hard and full of loss, no loss could compare with the death of his beloved son Joseph. Jacob's lament is an unavoidable human cry when death makes no sense and comfort does not come.

There is no life without loss. Jacob knew that truth very well. Loss is a central part of his story and ours. Because human beings are limited or finite creatures who love what will not last and possess what passes away, we will have grief for the losses that are inevitable in life. Men know grief for all the losses common in their lives: the death of a wife or parent or child, downsizing in the workplace, the end of a marriage, a disappointing defeat in an athletic contest, the loss of a dream or hope. For men today, as for Jacob long ago, one mark of faithfulness is the willingness to let go of the illusion of control and accept the inevitability and unpredictability of loss in life. *Men know grief.* That is not our problem. Rather, the grief of men is hidden and how men grieve is not always recognized, hence the presumption that men have difficulty expressing the grief they feel deeply. The intent of this chapter is to explore how men might become more competent sufferers by learning to grieve the losses they do not always understand and share the grief that is not easily comforted.

THE MALE DILEMMA ABOUT GRIEVING

I remember my grandfather as a sad man. He immigrated from Sweden in the 1890s and eventually homesteaded on the prairies of North Dakota. His wife, Emelia, died in childbirth in 1904 leaving him with three children under the age of four to raise on his own. My grandfather never married again and lived for fifty-seven years with buried guilt and grief for bringing fair Emelia from Sweden to die on the harsh plains of North Dakota. He was a simple man who lived silently and privately with his sorrow. My father never talked about growing up without a mother. He had learned well from my grandfather how to hide his grief. In a sense, the story of my grandfather is every man's story. The mark of being a man is to suffer in silence. Big boys don't cry. It is a sign of weakness. While this stereotype has been modified significantly, it is still difficult for men to share the pain of sadness.

In Pat Conroy's novel *Beach Music*, Jack McCall's wife, Shyla, committed suicide when their only child, Leah, was two years old. He was overtaken by a sadness that seemed permanent. Although he did not cry, he described the tears within him as an undiscovered and untouched inland sea. Jack's inability to grieve was similar to the way he loved. In a conversation with his mother when she is near death, he concludes that the only way he can love is in secret. "There's a deep, sourceless river I can tap into when no one else is near. But because it lies hidden and undiscovered, I can't lead expeditions to it. So I love strangely and obliquely. My love becomes a kind of guesswork. It brings no refreshment nor eases any pain."[1] This hidden river where love resides is like the inland sea of tears: it has no outlet. In order for men to find healing from their grief, they will need to find an outlet for this "inland sea of tears."

Because the grief of men is frequently hidden, the pains of loss are intensified by loneliness and isolation. So, for example, the loneliness and sadness of my grandfather were interchangeable. Jacob was also a solitary, perhaps lonely man surrounded by power and wealth. Men are often doubly disenfranchised when they experience loss. Men should not feel the pain *and* if they do, they should not share it with anyone. Or if men grieve, it takes a form that others do not recognize as mourning and again they are isolated. The bravado that men use to cover over grief also separates them from communities of care and the possibility of healing. As a result, male grief is often old and brittle. Leo Hall is a successful dentist and very alone in his life. His father died when he was two. After forty-three years, he is still depressed and angry about his father's death. But, he said, recently, "I don't let my wife or children or mother or stepfather know how utterly lonely I am." The emotional world in which Leo lives is that inland sea of tears without outlet.

I remember the feeling of panic that struck my soul as I watched [my wife] Lynda, my mother, [my four-year-old daughter] Diana Jane all die before my eyes. I remember the pandemonium that followed. . . . And I remember the realization sweeping over me that I would soon plunge into a darkness from which I might never again emerge as a sane, normal, believing man. . . . I learned gradually that the deeper we plunge into suffering, the deeper we can enter into a new, and different, life—a life no worse than before and sometimes better. . . . We can run from the darkness, or we can enter into the darkness and face the pain of loss. We can indulge ourselves in self-pity, or we can empathize with others and embrace their pains as our own. We can run away from sorrow and drown it in addictions, or we can learn to live with sorrow. . . . My own catastrophic loss thus taught me the incredible power of choice—to enter the darkness and to feel sorrow, as I did after the accident, even as I continued to work and to care for people, especially my children. . . . I knew that running from the darkness would only lead to greater darkness later on. I also knew that my soul had the capacity to grow—to absorb evil and good, to die and live again, to suffer abandonment and find God. In choosing to face the night, I took my first steps toward the sunrise.

Gerald L Sittser, *A Grace Disguised: How the Soul Grows Through Loss*

The stories of Jacob, my grandfather, Jack McCall, Leo Hall, and Gerald Sittser raise three important questions about men and grief. (1) What cultural stereotypes affect the ways in which men express or repress sadness? (2) For what do men grieve? What are the particular experiences of loss in our time that evoke and intensify the experience of grief in men? (3) What will help men grieve more fully? These questions will provide the framework for our reflections in this chapter. The freedom to grieve, however, is connected to many other changes men are experiencing in our time. What changes in how men think about their humanity will provide an outlet for the inland sea of sadness?

The process of separation from the mothering one evokes profound grief and anxiety for women and men alike. Leaving the physical and emotional unity of the first bond is both a necessary loss and an incurable wound that is replicated throughout life. For men, this ordinary grief has been intensified since the start of the Industrial Revolution. Because fathers are frequently absent from the home, boys must leave the safety of mother's world and enter father's realm of adventure and death without props and with little support from other men. Unacknowledged grief is at the core of male identity from the beginning of life. When boys must make this journey toward manhood alone because their fathers are absent, weak, preoccupied, or abusive, the grief is doubled. If smoldering rage and unchecked aggression among young men in this society is one consequence of hidden grief and isolation, the urgency for men to discover ways to mourn is also doubled.

OVERCOMING CULTURAL STEREOTYPES

Even if everyone agreed it is urgent for the sake of social order that men learn to grieve more effectively and even if men themselves acknowledged that the pain of loneliness and isolation accompanying hidden grief is unbearable, the obstacles impeding the development of new male responses to loss are still daunting. Among those obstacles are well-established expectations from the culture that support the strategies men use to effect contradictory goals: to connect with others and to hide from grief. Other chapters in this volume address some of the cultural stereotypes that must be overcome for men to grieve more easily. For example, as long as manliness is equated with *poise in the face of tragedy or composure in the midst of a crisis*, grief will be kept hidden so that male invincibility can retain its veneer. Men do not create this need for invincibility alone. Families that support control and rely on composure in fathers, husbands, and sons make grieving more difficult.

The inclination of men to fix things makes them useful around the house but it also complicates human intimacy. Men often use this *fix-it mode* in response to intense emotions or in the face of significant loss. It is a way to stay connected and be helpful without revealing vulnerable feelings. Samuel Osherson tells a poignant story of someone who came late for a men's retreat. He looked forlorn and upset when he arrived. Midway through the second day, the man admitted it was hard for him to be there because his brother, the troubled one in the family, had committed suicide the week before. His grief, shame, and anger were, Osherson reports, palpable but "he kept his feelings buried deep behind his manly facade of being the brother who takes care of others, without regard to himself."[2] Even when men want to experience grief, looking out for the needs of others and trying to fix things that are broken remain trusted patterns of responding to loss that are difficult to give up.

Becoming abstract or intellectual is another way for men to avoid being overwhelmed with the emotions of grief. When men intellectualize away the emotions of grief or provide abstract accounts of the loss, they want to connect with others without having to be vulnerable. More than anything else, the cultural myth that men should not be vulnerable determines the male response to loss. As a consequence, men do not learn how to talk about vulnerability, sorrow, or shame. They forget how to heal wounds that continue to ache, how to draw others close and not just drive them away, how to be more responsive to those they love. At the same time, men flinch from the connections they want when loss occurs in order to avoid acknowledging neediness. When men do share their grief, they quickly discover powerlessness and the reality that men have little to offer one another in times of emotional need. If the hidden river where loves resides has no outlet, neither then does the inland river of grief. For that reason, learning to love and learning to grieve are reciprocal.

Possession has often accompanied the need for control in men. Having things, a wife, status, or a garage full of machines is one way that power is measured and a man's worth is determined. It is also a way of denying the reality of human finitude. Things are easier to possess than people, which may explain in part the attraction of men to tractors, cars, and gadgets. And if what we own is thought of as a buffer against death, then the more we own, the safer we are. It is not surprising, therefore, that the aphorism "whoever has the most toys in the end wins" has been used to describe the centrality of possession for men. When possessing becomes the pervasive form of male control in a consumerist society, *holding on to or possessing people or things* easily becomes a way of life.

Theologian Arthur McGill has observed that in the kingdom of God, "there is simply no such thing as *possession*. We do not possess ourselves; we constantly *receive* ourselves and *expend* ourselves."[3] The new identity we have in Christ challenges all living through possessions. It is not wrong to have goods but possessing makes it harder to understand that we have life as a gift to give it away. We are challenged to let go of living by possessing. If we learn to be generous, acknowledge contingency and death, we will discover we are stronger when we wait than when we possess. We have our life as a gift.

Accepting vulnerability as part of being human is a necessary prelude to men grieving more freely. Vulnerability is a constant theme in this book. If it is not masculine to be emotional, powerless to fix things, or vulnerable, then men will spend time, energy, and sometimes considerable money to eliminate vulnerability. Philip Culbertson, in his book *Counseling Men*, describes the male dilemma: "Patriarchal masculinity denigrates and trivializes the world of inner experience, feeling, and intuition. This inner world is deemed weak, making men too vulnerable."[4]

The transformation of cultural stereotypes that still lock men into grief-impeding behavior is the most difficult, daunting challenge before us. Men cannot effect that transformation alone because men alone did not invent the stereotypes. It is work women and men must do together. Because these strategies for avoiding the work of grieving are learned, they can of course be unlearned as well. Men will be free to modify these strategies only when they are able to reject the cultural myths about masculinity that undergird them.

THE MANY GRIEFS OF MEN

Loss is not gender specific. Neither is grief. When a child loses a pet, or a son or daughter leaves home, when a person is fired or a friend moves away, when a marriage ends in divorce or a parent dies, the loss is real for both women and men. The meaning of the loss varies widely, however. The meaning of the loss depends on the value ascribed to what has been lost or the significance of the relationship with the lost person or object. For those who prize possessions highly, for example, the loss of things like cars, investment bonds, or treasured books may be the occasion for grief that is surprising in its intensity. It is impossible in this short chapter to examine all the stories men tell about grief in their lives. I have chosen only a few losses that men tell about most often, find the most difficult to share, or identify as the hardest to get over.[5]

The Loss of Childhood

The death of a parent early in life often means the end of childhood for both boys and girls. If a father dies or if parents divorce when a boy is young, the boy is often expected to assume responsibilities prematurely in the absence of a father. The loss of a father or the dream of belonging to a happy family is shattered but so is the innocence of childhood. Ronald described his losses in and of childhood with these words:

I was inducted into the status of pallbearer at age eleven. My sister died of scarlet fever and my closest childhood friend died of poliomyelitis. These losses, and other less serious deprivations in my early life, culminated in the accidental death of my father. I was a man before I had finished being a boy. The "things of a child" were put away in order to survive. I did not recover my lost boyhood even though I played around irresponsibly after my divorce. I would not have known this about my life, however, if I had not been invited and then coerced to rehearse stories of grief.

We hurry childhood in many ways in this society. The kind of information available in the media and on the Web means that children know more and more earlier and earlier. Children are expected to participate in activities organized by adults that redefine childhood play. When a death or divorce occurs in a family, the temptation is to redefine the roles of those who remain so that "things can stay pretty much the same" even though a systemic loss has occurred. Children who grow up in urban poverty and street violence lose the innocence of childhood. "Becoming a man before being a boy" is one of the unnecessary consequences of early parental death, divorce, and the regular experience of senseless violence. Creating a safe space for children to mourn not only emphasizes the need for children to grieve; it reminds us they need to be protected when possible from losing childhood as well.

Boys who experience significant loss have already learned to stifle emotions and maintain silence. Anger is deflected, sadness is hidden, and guilt for being the survivor is repressed. As a result, the grief is locked in the past in ways that limit thinking about the future in hopeful ways. Richard told me his story this way:

> I was eight when my father died. He had never been sick. When my mother told us he had died, my six-year-old brother started crying. I told him to shut up. I only allowed myself to cry when I was alone. Everyone told me I had to be strong because I was the "man of the house." I remember waiting in the driveway for weeks and weeks, hoping he would come back. Even now, thirty years after his death, I often get unpredictably sad driving home from work. When the grief is sequestered in the past, hope and the future are hidden as well. We dare not overlook the absence of hope in men who have never grieved or resolved childhood loss.

Richard's story demonstrates how easy it is for boys to learn not to grieve. Adults who want to protect children from the pain of loss contribute to the denial by hiding their own grief from children or withholding information about the loss. Boys like adults to say they are strong and give them special privileges because of it. The effect on children is opposite of what is intended. They become more confused in their grief, more confirmed in their guilt, more isolated in their sadness. Richard had to be strong because he was prematurely expected to assume the duties of adult manhood. When a child loses the parent of the same gender, it is much too common for relatives and friends or the surviving parent to promote the child to a replacement role in the family, depriving the child of age-appropriate behavior.

The Loss of a Spouse

A man's response to the death of a spouse has been described with force and vulnerability by C. S. Lewis in *A Grief Observed*. Reading the book, we are in touch with unmanageable emotions, our interdependence on one another in marriage, and the fact that grief is the cost of loving. After living most of his life as a single person, C. S. Lewis had married Joy Gresham. Joy died of cancer not long after they were married. *A Grief Observed* contains four notebooks that Lewis wrote as part of his grieving. His reflections begin with rage at God as a "cosmic sadist" and conclude with a recognition that we live with the mystery of God as the "great iconoclast" who continues to shatter our expectations of how life should be. He is aware of being an embarrassment to his friends. "At work, at the club, in the street, I see people, as they approach me, trying to make up their minds whether they'll 'say something about it' or not. I hate it if they do, and if they don't."[6] And in the end, he admits that we cannot understand the mysteries of life and death. We can only know the pains of absence.

> Her absence is like the sky, spread over everything. But no, that is not quite accurate. There is one place where her absence comes locally home to me, and it is a place I can't avoid. I mean my own body. It had such a different importance while it was the body of Joy's lover. Now it's like an empty house. . . . I know that the thing I want is exactly the thing I can never get. The old life, the jokes, the drinks, the arguments, the love-making, the tiny, heartbreaking commonplace. . . . And that, just that, is what I cry out for, with mad, midnight endearments and entreaties spoken into the empty air.[7]

Although the imagery that Lewis uses to describe his own grief after Joy's death is immoderate, emotionally charged, and highly evocative of our own grief, writing in notebooks rather than ranting with friends continues the male mode of private grieving. If the grief is privately expressed through a journal or to stones by the river, it is easier to maintain the male image of control. The expression of grief is carefully moderated even though the loss is felt deeply.

When the loss of a wife is because of divorce, shame and rage are added to emptiness. Because of the shame, men hide the grief of divorce, too often until the rage is no longer manageable. Grieving the loss of a wife is complicated by the worry of men about living alone. It is generally agreed that widowers are regularly at greater risk for adverse health consequences than widows. Apprehension about managing on their own is added to the aching emptiness in men who grieve the loss of a wife.

Absent Fathers and the Loss of Blessing

Over centuries, men have been absent from the home for many reasons and fathers have been distant from their children for equally diverse circumstances. Not so long ago in this society, the prototype of the absent father was the corporate executive or busy professional who left for work before the children were awake and returned from work after they had gone to bed. The marriage was intact but mother was a single parent. Sons knew their fathers at a distance. Then the focus shifted to deadbeat dads, men who do not pay child support or who have otherwise abandoned responsibility for their children. Visiting fathers struggle not to perpetuate a pattern of distance because they are absent from the home.

Some sons, of course, have never known their biological father. The birth father may be pictured by the child's mother as someone the son would not want to know. In such circumstances, the grief for the absent father is covered over by the mother's rage or magnified by idealizations. This pattern of idealizing is particularly common when a father dies when the son is very young. Children who are separated from their fathers through divorce may even idealize the man who abandons them. When a boy loses a parent, he creates a myth of that parent in order to endure the grief. The grief is particularly painful when the fatherless family is an exception in society. When nobody's father comes to the piano recital or the sport's banquet, the negative impact on the child may still be significant but the grief is diminished.

When fathers are physically absent, it is easy for blessings to be withheld or simply overlooked. When fathers are present, they may still withhold blessing their sons because their fathers had never blessed them, because pride is a dangerous sin to be avoided and unseemly in children, or both. While I am absolutely certain that my father was proud of me, he never said so. It was a matter of Christian piety and his relationship to his father. The following moment in my life illustrates the close connection between grief for our fathers and the longing for a blessing. My wife and I celebrated our twenty-fifth wedding anniversary by taking our children and their significant others at that time to a performance of *Les Miserables* in the elegant Chicago Theatre. We had seats in the fourth row. At the conclusion of the musical, when the father, Jean Valjean, sings a blessing to his daughter, Cosette, and her lover, Marius, I began to sob uncontrollably. It did not take me long to connect my tears with hearing my father's voice for the first time in four years on our wedding tape at breakfast that morning. I was crying for my father. But even more, I was crying for a blessing I had never received. It is the deepest hole in my life.

When Middle-Aged Sons Lose a Parent

The death of parents often has a significant impact on middle-aged sons. Some adult sons feel abandoned when a parent dies. They are like orphans. Some are frustrated or guilty because they had postponed dealing with unfinished business with a parent until it was too late. Ten years after his father's death, Edwardo still chastises himself for taking too long to get to his parents for a visit. His grief is not only for his father who died but for the three choices he made that day that prevented him from seeing his father and saying "I love you" one more time. Sometimes the death of a father or a mother is the occasion for sons to claim the autonomy they could not exercise as long as the parent was alive.

When a parent's death is the prelude to freedom, the grieving may stop. The catalyst for what we often describe as a midlife crisis may be the death of the parent who was the inhibitor of impulses. Freedom becomes license. Because the middle years are tainted with loss, a parent's death may occur when a company is downsizing or when older sons begin to have health problems that are also a sign of aging. Men may withdraw from the relationships that sustain them in order to avoid the awareness of finiteness.

The buffer is gone when the last parent dies. For men who have been working hard to avoid finiteness, the death of a parent is often a double loss and a traumatic blow. They lose a parent but they also lose a buffer between themselves and death. The last parent's death is a reminder to adult sons (and daughters, of course) that they are next in succession to die. Both of my parents died before I turned fifty. Since I am the oldest of sixteen cousins, I took some comfort at that time that both my father and mother had living siblings. Now they are all gone, many having lived well into their nineties. In my extended family, I am next. We all work out some little trick to keep death at a distance. But the death of a parent is an unmistakable sign that finitude is unavoidable and death is a little nearer.

Loss in the Workplace

Work-related grief is complicated. It is difficult enough for a man to tell his family and friends that he is out of work. There are dimensions related to the job loss itself that are difficult to talk about: shame to be out of work, anger at the way it happened, sadness about losing a dream, isolation out of fear that no one wants to hear about what may happen to them next. The grief is intensified when it is not shared and the grieving is prolonged when the sadness must be hidden.

> When work goes sour, there is *grief*, just as surely as when you lose a loved one or your health. We know a lot about ways to handle the grief when someone dies. This can help us learn how to handle the grief when our work turns deadening, killing. . . . The healing miracle of grief work, when it happens, as it inevitably must, is in holding together as one reality life and death, hope and disappointment, connection and separation, trust and betrayal. Somehow, in good grief work, there is simultaneous investment and withdrawal, a claim and a letting go, a yes and a no, both hearty.
>
> James E. Dittes,
> *Men at Work: Life beyond the Office*

It is not easy for men to share their sadness in the workplace because the risks of being vulnerable are too high. Nonetheless, men need companions from their place of work *who understand what they are going through* and who will listen to their story and hold their grief. For some men, the pain of despair over losses in the workplace is so intense and the fear of losing everything so profound that they dare not let go of the grief because it is all they have. Everything becomes flat and meaningless, gray in color. To care for men experiencing loss in the workplace we must avoid two unhelpful responses: (1) we should not take away the grief prematurely because we are tired of the sadness or because we want to fix the grief; and (2) we should not encourage them to nurse the anger related to the loss in ways that prevent them from moving toward the future in hope.

Jeffrey is overwhelmed by a number of losses that were mostly hidden from view.

> I am a Vietnam veteran with a master's degree that does not seem to count for much anymore. Almost every position I apply for is swallowed up by women and minorities. I used to have a family, two

kids, a dog, two cars, insurance, self-respect, and a little piece of land by a lake. Now I have a new wife who earns more than I do, lots of debt, and occasional work. I should be grateful but I'm not. I fought to protect my country but I cannot provide for my family. It is hard for me to know who I am.

The grief men like Jeffrey feel today because of the inability to get jobs, an unexpected job loss, or the failure to get an expected promotion is exaggerated by the loss of preferred status in this society. In one sense, this loss of assumed privilege is common to men of all races. In other respects, Ellis Cose has observed, race is relevant. African American men are not "as exercised as white men about the decline of male power and privilege, since most don't believe they had very much of either to begin with."[8] For African American men, it is the loss of a dream that brings grief covered with cynicism and despair. If, however, a man grew up believing he was entitled to be at the head of the line or at least in the line, the loss of privileged status is also a painful internal transaction.

Affirmative action has been a necessary exaggeration in recent times to rectify a legacy of injustice that gave preference to white males in a variety of situations. As a result, some men have not gotten jobs or promotions that would have been automatically theirs a few decades ago. Few would disagree with Cose "that being a male, at least a white male, in American society has historically come with certain privileges."[9] Even for those who agree it is necessary for white males to lose their preferred status in order to correct centuries of injustice against women and minority persons, the loss of preferred status is still a source of grief. From the perspective of those who are powerless, the white man's lament seems trivial. Suffering, however, is always in the eyes of the beholder. We need to be able to care for men who mourn the loss of privilege that should have been taken from them long ago.

HELPING MEN TO GRIEVE

For men the principle psychological barrier to grieving is the inability to acknowledge vulnerability. As a result, men do not know how to develop strategies for coping with loss that acknowledge their need for others when they have been emotionally wounded. The inability to understand human creatureliness as finite and dependent is a major theological barrier to grieving. Men need to discover a different view of being human in order to be more open to the gift of grieving. At the same time, men need to practice grieving. The cultural stereotypes that limit the range of emotional expression for men will only be modified as men try new ways of responding to loss.

Finding Common Ground for Grieving

Beyond changing the way they think about being human, men need to recognize the patterns of responding to loss that limit their freedom to grieve. Some of those patterns of traditional male behavior are essential to conducting a workable, effective life. As such, they are difficult to change. Men in grief readily agree that it is both frightening and freeing to relinquish the constricting aspects of traditional male behavior. In order to make the changes necessary to be free to grieve, men need to agree that (1) grieving is a part of living because loss is an inescapable dimension of life; and (2) the reason for grieving is not to weaken life but to strengthen it.

Helping men deal with loss begins by finding safe, common ground in which they are free to grieve in their own way and at their own pace in the company of accepting friends. Generally, an all-male group provides the most comfortable common ground for responding to loss. Old male patterns of dealing with intense feelings do not fade quickly. Some men need freedom to grieve silently for a long time even though they might not want to be alone in that silence. At the same time, we should not discourage appropriate attempts to make men in grief more comfortable with constructive patterns of grieving previously prohibited by male cultural stereotypes.

It is a mistake to equate crying with mourning. Although shedding tears is an effective release of sadness, it is not the sole one. People express their sadness and hurt in other ways besides crying. Moreover, sadness is not the only issue in grief. Anger, shame, fear, loneliness, emptiness, and bewilderment are all aspects of grief for which crying may not be the best release. All-male grief groups will seek to establish comfortable common ground so that participants are more likely to discuss issues regarding the fear of loss of control, discuss sexual concerns, and release feelings in an environment that allows tears among men. Finding this common ground is one way of diminishing the need for the counterproductive strategies identified earlier that inhibit men from beginning the work of grieving.

Making Friends to Grieve With

Encouraging people to grieve presupposes that there are people who will listen to the story of loss and hear the pains of grief. One of the major impediments to grieving for anyone is the absence of empathic companions. This is a particular dilemma for men because they seldom form relationships that include emotional sharing. Traditionally, men have built relationships around doing something together. When men who have suffered loss are asked what they want from a friendship with another man, the qualities they most frequently name are acceptance, honesty, and understanding. Henry told this story about friends in grief.

> My daughter was sixteen when she committed suicide. I could not go to work. I was hurt, angry, ashamed, and confused. I do not know how I would have survived her death without two friends who listened to me rage and cry without judging or trying to take away my pain. Sometimes, they just sat with me when I needed to be silent. I have thought many times since how fortunate I am to have two friends. Too many men I know would have been alone with their grief.

Henry knew the gift of friendship when he needed to grieve. When we have friends we know will listen to our pain without judging, who will accept our few tears without insisting on more, and who are trustworthy with our vulnerability, then we will be free to grieve freely. Ideally, we will have friends to turn to when grief comes. Sometimes, we make friends with those who honor us with their faithful listening presence. Either way, men cannot endure grief without friends.

The Church As a Community of the Suffering Ones

Grief isolates. All creatures tend to retreat into themselves and heal their wounds in private. Men are no exception. Everything we know about grieving, however, counters that impulse. We need another's hand to find our way out of the darkness. Finding hope again after an experience of loss is an act of mutuality. It is the experience of mutuality that transforms our dread of abandonment and our terrors of isolation into communities of suffering ones. Whenever men gather in congregations, whether to fix the roof or count money, it is an opportunity to share joys and sadness, honor celebrations and begin grieving, and thereby build a community of the suffering ones.

SHARING POWER

Having the family blessing was power in the biblical world. It promised both prominence and dominance. When Isaac blessed Jacob, thinking it was Esau, he said:

> May God give you of the dew of heaven,
> and of the fatness of the earth,
> and plenty of grain and wine.
> Let peoples serve you,
> and nations bow down to you.
> Be lord over your brothers,
> and may your mother's sons
> bow down to you.
> Cursed be everyone who curses you,
> and blessed be everyone who
> blesses you!
>
> (Gen. 27:28–29)

In order to achieve that kind of power, Jacob had first persuaded Esau to give up his birthright and then, with the help of his mother, Rebekah, gained the blessing of old, blind Isaac by deceit. This incident that marks Jacob for life is the story of a man influenced by his mother's ambitions for him and carried away into deceit and theft.

Only one son in a family could have that kind of power and influence. When Esau discovered that his twin brother had tricked him out of his father's blessing, he pleaded with Isaac: Bless me, me also, father! It was not possible. Jacob had been made lord even over Esau, the rightful heir to the blessing. The deed was done and Isaac could not undo the word of blessing he had given. Instead, Isaac tells Esau that his home must be "away from the fatness of the earth" and "away from the dew of heaven."

> By your sword you shall live,
>> and you shall serve your brother;
> but when you break loose,
>> you shall break his yoke from your neck.
>> (Gen. 27:40)

It is difficult to imagine the pain that both Esau and Isaac felt when they discovered how Jacob had tricked them. Esau had been his father's favorite but now Jacob had all the power. The way the story is told, we are not surprised by this deception. "Jacob" means "supplanter." Eventually, Jacob believed it was his destiny to take his place as a true successor to his grandfather Abraham. In the beginning, however, he used deceit to gain power that belonged to Esau. "Supplanter" is an accurate image for the ways in which men have assumed the right to undermine or take over the power of others for the sake of domination.

The cultivation of the land, the development of cities, and the conquest of enemies through war have all depended on the physical strength of men. Men plowed fields, fought wars, built railroads, dug graves, and forged steel because they were physically strong. The myths of manhood frequently celebrated the power in men derived from physical strength. Emotional strength was neither expected nor encouraged in men. Because physical strength is not required for much of the labor that must be done today, there is new potential for equality between women and men in the workplace and the home. Men are now free to complement their physical strength with emotional strength. That is not an easy task, however, because emotional strength is gained by living with vulnerability. Men have used physical power to promote their invulnerability. In order to redefine masculinity and power, men need to practice living with vulnerability in a more constructive way.

British sociologist Arthur Brittan has made a helpful distinction between the essence of being a man (sometimes referred to as "masculinity") and *masculism*, "the ideology that justifies and naturalizes male domination."[1] In his book *Masculinity and Power*, Brittan argues that hierarchy, domination, and competitiveness are all related to each other and that the exercise of male power can best be understood in terms of the relationship of these three dimensions of human relatedness. Furthermore, the descriptions of manhood and the presumptions of domination promoted by *masculism* are resistant to change even though they vary over time and among differing contexts. *Masculism* tends to give primacy to the conviction that gender definitions are not negotiable even when men know those definitions are socially constructed. The political domination of men is promoted, the subordination of women is assumed, and the power of men is taken for granted in public spheres and in the family.

Having power has been a primary way of defining being a man. Gathering power through blessings, wealth, trickery, position, or from some other form of achievement has been a mark of manhood since the time of Jacob and before. Possessions enhance a sense of masculine power, and holding to positions of power continues to be regarded by many men as a male right. For modern men who are married, the issue of power often comes down to a simple issue: who controls the television remote. The desire for power has led some men to patterns of domination or violence that have impeded the development of fundamental dimensions of being human. Respect for others, humility, collaboration, and sacrifice are still regarded by too many men as contrary to their version of *masculism*. This assumption of power has continued along with privilege as rights of manhood. As long as men think of hierarchies of power or having "power over," then learning to share power is a stiff challenge.

WHAT IS POWER?

"Power is the capacity of some persons to produce intended and foreseen effects on others."[2] That definition by sociologist Dennis Wrong suggests that the aim of power is to influence or have an effect. There are instances when that influence is not intended. An individual's life may be transformed by reading about the charitable acts of an

anonymous person. Most of the time, however, we use power intentionally to effect change or influence or control others. There are at least four different ways power is used, each of which can be illustrated by the Jacob story: power based on *force or might*, power through *manipulation*, power by *persuasion*, and power exercised by people in *authority*.

- Laban had *legitimate authority* over Jacob as the uncle who took him in when Jacob was a fugitive and the father of the woman Jacob desperately wanted to marry. Jacob accepted the power of Laban and worked hard to diminish Laban's power by becoming more successful and wealthy.

- When Esau traded his birthright to Jacob for a bowl of porridge, both trickery and persuasion were used. Jacob *persuaded* Esau to believe that a birthright would be of no use if he were dead. As is often the case, Esau felt he had been duped once his hunger was gone and he realized he had squandered his birthright for a bowl of porridge.

- Jacob's *deception* of Isaac to receive the blessing due to Esau is a classic illustration of manipulative use of power. Laban also abandoned his legitimate authority for the sake of manipulative power by changing the rules about counting spotted goats.

- Jacob's fear of Esau's anger and *physical power* profoundly affected Jacob's life and kept him on the run. Jacob hoped that the gifts he brought would persuade Esau not to use the military force he had at his disposal. The presence of force, even if it is never used, is often enough to influence behavior.

In itself, power is good. It is the ability to act or be acted upon. When we understand power in psychological terms, it generally refers to internal strength to speak or make things happen. Personal power enables individuals to make decisions, pursue dreams, and resist abuse. The power to speak is central for human development. Social power may diminish the personal power of individuals through the threat of punishment, violence, manipulation, or coercion. One of the gender tensions today is that men may say they feel personally powerless while women still experience the privileged positions of patriarchy as "power over." Men may feel powerless because their freedom to dominate has been restricted in order to increase the freedom of women and other marginalized persons to be empowered with personal autonomy. While their loss is real, men must relinquish presumptions of dominance if we are to establish human communities of trust where women and men share power equally. Although the abuse of power around the globe takes many forms, it is still mostly carried out by men. Because the abuse of power remains so pervasive and so violent, it is the most serious issue in human existence today.

WHEN POWER IS A PROBLEM

It should not be difficult for men today to identify how the misuse of power in the Jacob story is mirrored in modern life. The discussion of aggression and violence in another chapter describes how common it is for men to use force to gain revenge, control, or sex. When men feel powerless, they may use force simply to reassert their domination and control. The catalogue of deceptions has moved from goats in the story of Jacob to today's grand schemes to swindle people eager to acquire riches quickly. Trickery abounds. On U.S. college campuses, one of the more insidious illustrations of the abuse of power is a drug put secretly in a woman's drink in order to diminish or eliminate altogether her resistance to sexual advance. Such drugging is often the prelude to date rape. Because the exercise of legitimate authority has been so contaminated by deception, corruption, and the abuse of power, it is easy to conclude that the positive use of power is a practice underdeveloped in men.

Power is a problem in life when it drives us toward control to avoid the limits of being human. Control also has a positive dimension because it invites full participation in human communities. When we say that an individual is "in charge of his life," we imply that he is exercising power appropriately to respond to the challenges and opportunities he experiences. Control is used too often, however, to dominate others and deny our mortality. In order to stay in control, we will devise strategies that avoid or ignore signs of finitude. When we "play it safe" to "avoid risk," we flee from life to avoid death. When we seek to control others to enhance our own status and eliminate death from awareness, we violate others and isolate ourselves in order to avoid death.

Sexual and physical violence by men toward women and children is a tragic sign of the continuing need of men to have "power over" someone or something in order to feel power within. James Poling has written courageously about the abuse of power through sexual violence. "Those who have experienced sexual violence are the victims of abuse of power. Children are vulnerable to adult abuse of power because they lack understanding and resources for self-protection. . . . Women are vulnerable to assault and manipulation because of the power of men."3 Parents hit children to establish their authority. Men hit women to show them who is boss. In its ideal expression, power is the energy of life that mobilizes us to fashion sustaining and empowering webs for living. When power is abused, those relational webs are destroyed and the possibility of human community is severely limited.

I have already suggested that the close connection between potency or power and vulnerability in male anatomy is a metaphor for what men need to learn about being human. The prostate is not only a source of male potency: it is the place of greatest vulnerability to cancer in men. Prostate cancer is unsettling emotionally for men precisely because we are vulnerable at the source of our potency. The primary purpose of the prostate is to produce the thick fluid that is part of semen. Because treatment for prostate cancer eliminates the production of semen and sometimes diminishes the capacity for an erection, it is often difficult for men to speak of an illness that touches so close to our presumed locus of potency and male identity. On the other hand, the prostate is the physical place in the male body *most* susceptible to cancer. Having prostate cancer became for me tangible evidence of personal vulnerability. If I understand myself as a finite, contingent creature in God's care, then I am more likely to share my vulnerability and avoid abusing others.

A Personal Story of Power and Marriage

About twenty years ago, my wife, Phyllis, was asked to reflect on marriage and family living at a retreat for women. Her reflections were candid and even now are painful for me to read. I include her comments about me and about men in general even though they are not flattering because they reflect common perceptions of men by women and subtle ways men abuse power in marriage.

> After two years, I had a picture-book marriage and I was miserable. Herbert had taken the lead just as I had hoped he would and as my mother had hoped before me. He not only took power, I gave it away. I threw my power at him and hated him for it. I thought men ran the world because they were smarter and better. I had given over all responsibility and power to Herbert and he wasn't perfect. I did not like the prospect of spending the rest of my life propping up a fallible human being. . . . When our children were eight and ten, I went away for two months. Instead of helping me, Herbert had full responsibility caring for the children and the house. Everything changed. We discovered he was more willing to take over than I was ready to give up what had been my territory. Before long, Herbert had pretty well taken over the house and the kids. He became so enthusiastic about

my career, he nearly took that over too. When I was finally ordained, Herbert got scared. When he said that the next move was to where I got a job, I got scared. Roles had changed radically but in some ways we were the same. I became aware that I was still my mother's little girl and he was the first-born pastor's son who was used to running the show. We had come miles and had miles to go.

These reflections illustrate two fundamental truths about women, men, and power: (1) women have been socialized for centuries to give over power to men; and (2) most men are inclined, as I obviously was, to take over whenever they can. Sometimes, in order to prop up a fallible or weak man, women give the appearance of giving over power even though they must provide the stability for a family unit. There is, however, a deeper and more challenging conclusion I draw from thinking about my own actions: love does not guarantee justice in marriage. Husbands will declare their love for their wives, as I would, while at the same time continuing to act as if the bond is not a relationship of equals.

Pauline Kleingeld has written about justice in marriage in this way. "In order to promote justice in marriage, the social perception of the essence of marriage must be changed in such a way that the ideal of marriage is conceived of as not only a matter of love, but also of justice. . . . If the cultural understanding of marriage changed in this way, this would mean, first, that couples would understand themselves not only as communities of love, but also as communities of free and interdependent equals who treat each other in accordance with principles of justice."[4] This proposal would fundamentally change the basis for sharing power in marriage. Love is not enough. Nor can we assume that mutual regard alone will establish a just bond. Working for a just and equal sharing of power in the roles and responsibilities of marriage must become part of the covenant bond and the common goal of life that couples share together.

Sharing power in a marriage is about mutuality of influence. Wives are more likely to accept their husband's influence, even in an unstable marriage. Husbands are less willing to admit influence. Wives often get what they want by manipulating the situation so that husbands think it was their idea. The situation may be as simple as a husband turning off the football game in order to talk with his wife about a troubling phone call from her mother. Such action demonstrates a husband's commitment to "us" as well as "me." A response like "Can't it wait until halftime or the end of the game?" communicates the opposite value. If "giving in" to a wife's influence is perceived by a husband as "giving up" power, then it is a zero sum game. An unequal balance of power is deadly to marriage. Sharing power in marriage begins quite simply with the acknowledgment of mutuality of influence.

Power is a great gift in marriage if it is shared. When everyone is empowered to speak and influence choices that are made, love flows more freely and conflicts are settled more quickly. When power is out of balance, then decisions about who initiates sex, how money is spent, how clean the bathrooms are and who cleans them, which relative to visit at Christmas, or the use of leisure time are frequently occasions for anger, hurt, or both. Someone who insists that "I may not always be right, but I am never wrong" is an unlikely candidate for sharing power. Even under the most positive circumstances, however, sharing power in marriage is a complex process that requires trust, the willingness to be wrong, and the capacity to accommodate.

IMPEDIMENTS TO SHARING POWER

The exercise of power in relationships of trust fosters individual growth and strengthens communal bonds. We are in a wonderfully creative time for men and women alike to fashion new patterns of sharing power in order to enhance the fullness of being human. It is a complex time as well because new patterns of sharing power evoke long-standing assumptions of male dominance and deep resistance to change. The practice of power in personal and social contexts often reveals the darker and more destructive aspects of being a man. Power is used to dominate, violate, or control rather than to empower for the sake of individual growth and communal wholeness. There are, therefore, several impediments to learning to share power that must be acknowledged if men are to envision new possibilities for just communities of women and men.

Dominion over the earth rather than partnership has dominated our understanding of creation. As long as we presume that humankind has a biblical mandate to have dominion over creation, "power over" or domination has legitimacy. Recent biblical scholarship of the Creation stories in Genesis suggests greater partnership between humankind and the created order. In a very complex and subtle way, we are being called to share power with the environment by allowing the fragility of creation to influence daily decisions we make. We have explored this theme in the chapter on "nurturing" around the ancient notion of husbandry. If partnership is the biblical mandate for humans in relation to creation, sharing power must become the norm for relations between women and men within creation.

> In the Western world, the importance of self-reliant, individual action is systematically inculcated in males. To be masculine requires not only self-reliance and self-control, but control over other people and resources.
>
> Jean Lipman-Blumen,
> *Gender Roles and Power*

Men have assumed that having power eliminates the susceptibility to being wounded. Whenever men presume to be invulnerable in the exercise of power, it is easy to treat with disdain what cannot wound. It is only a small step from there to conclude that any acknowledgment of influence increases vulnerability. Two family sayings illustrate how difficult it is to increase one's vulnerability by sharing power: "You cannot sit on the hill and feel the breeze on your face unless you own the hill." "If you are not the lead dog, the scenery never changes." The result of invulnerability is self-sufficiency and isolation on top of the hill that in turn makes sharing power more difficult.

Sharing power includes sacrifice. The issue of accommodation or compromise is a volatile topic between the genders. We have assumed for much too long that women would be willing to sacrifice whatever the situation because it was their "nature." We know better now but that has not made it easy to change our gender expectations. As a result, women have been resistant to sacrifice for fear that they will be recast in an old and debilitating role. Men need to be very explicit about their commitment to compromise and accommodation that are an inevitable part of sharing power in order to find new ways to be together with women in the home and at work. Justice in relationships requires the redistribution of influence or control. In order to maintain justice in marriage and other relationships, mutual sacrifice is necessary. Mutual regard between persons in a relationship will enhance the possibility of sacrifice.

The inability to share power undermines friendship. We can all think about friendships that have deteriorated when giving gifts was one-sided. If the dominant principle governing an individual's life is to avoid indebtedness, then power in a friendship will not be shared easily because one person or couple will never be in debt. When a friend always reciprocates a gift or a generous gesture immediately, it is usually a sign that being indebted is too much like powerlessness and to be avoided as often as possible. Learning to experience the mutuality of friendship is another way to practice sharing power.

The inability to share power makes an idol out of money. In the mind of many, having money is having power. Controlling the money is also having even more power. Studies have shown that money is a major source of conflict in marriage. In order to avoid conflict, partners in a relationship will not always tell the truth about how much money they have spent. If a family or an organization has modest means but one person determines how much money is spent and for what, he or she is not sharing power. Making a budget to which everyone agrees and to which everyone is equally obligated is one way to balance power around money. Money will remain a source of tension in human relationships as long as it is linked to power and power is not shared.

The inability to share power breeds contempt. It is much too easy to treat with disdain those who are weak or cannot wound us. I agree with the suggestion that the origin of contempt toward children that leads to violence is because children are small, weak, and needy. If children are seen as not yet fully human, then it is not surprising that men hold them in contempt or are not eager to understand their needs, pains, or joys. In fact, anyone who is small, weak, or needy is held in contempt by a society controlled by men who glorify size, strength, and self-sufficiency. Contempt for the powerless leads to the oppression of the disadvantaged or vulnerable as well as the abuse of children.

LEARNING THE ART OF SHARING POWER

Heal hearts broken by the abuse of power. Over the last decades, we have discovered that it is not enough to disrupt male dominance without a parallel move toward self-awareness and empowerment for women and men alike. It is also increasingly clear that what we have been doing to transform men who abuse power has not worked well enough. When my wife, Phyllis, observed that she was frightened by my promise to follow her career, she was acknowledging how women, as well as men, participate in the brokenness of patriarchy. Rita Nakashima Brock has proposed an evocative approach to transforming the abuse of power. "I am seeking to turn patriarchy inside out, to reveal its ravaged, faint, fearful, broken heart, and to illuminate the power that heals heart."[5] When we turn the patriarchal heart "inside out," we acknowledge that brokenheartedness is within individuals (women as well as men), in relationships, and in social systems. Before hearts can be tutored, they must be healed. Before a heart can be healed, there must be a recognized need for healing. For men, this begins by admitting that the patriarchal heart is fearful and broken and probably always has been, at least since Jacob.

Take time to share power. It is difficult to share power when there is little or no time to negotiate. Whose time is more valuable, who has the most flexibility around time, and who mismanages time may be issues in the struggle for power. We have all rejected, internalized, or in some way modified maxims from our origins about the perception of time and the value of punctuality. If "haste makes waste," then the early bird may not get the worm. "Better to be five minutes early than ten minutes late" works only if "a stitch in time saves nine." Negotiating time to talk about concrete ways of sharing power may sometimes be the first moments in the process.

Take the long view. Power is seldom equally shared in every moment. Sometimes it is necessary for one person to have more power or influence in a relationship at a particular moment in order to accomplish a task or make a decision. We need to trust that power, like privilege and responsibility, will balance out in the long haul. If we need to keep score in order to maintain justice, it will be difficult to share power. Taking the long view also means that we take enough time to see the uniqueness of another for the sake of justice. Sharing power in marriage and in the workplace presumes a willingness to see the wholeness and fullness of a spouse for the sake of justice.

Sharing power leads to conflict. When men and women make a commitment to form just communities in which power is shared, they will inevitably experience unexpected conflicts and unseen impediments. In order to share power, men need to postpone gratification, express wishes clearly, negotiate and renegotiate promises made, and develop a short-term memory that is not always keeping score. Sharing power must include the practice of reconciliation in order to restore relationships broken by conflicts over contending views of what is right and just for women and men. Such a reconciliation cannot be achieved in haste. Nor can it overlook past hurts or past presumptions. If men and women can tend toward reconciliation and justice, they will find new ways to share power for the common good of home and the workplace.

Learn to honor resistance. Respect for resistance is a way of sharing power. Resistance is a form of counterpower that seeks to challenge the abuse of power whenever it occurs. Sometimes resistance looks like stubbornness or dogged determination. When it is oppression or domination that evokes resistance, then resistance is a sign of hope and faith to be honored. When men are determined to get their way in marriage, the strategy is to "wear them out" or "wear them down" if they (wives) give in to the demands. If our aim is to establish just relationships in which power is shared, men need to honor resistance as a way to justice. Resistance is an act of creative freedom and vitality if the aim is liberation and justice for all the people of God. If men learn to honor resistance, they will be less likely to wear resistance down with relentless pursuit. Men may find themselves siding with odd forms of resistance that seek to preserve life in the face of oppression.

Practice being vulnerable. For a long time, men have presumed power without susceptibility to being wounded. I have said it before but it bears repeating. Presuming invulnerability isolates. Because the human creature is essentially communal, hiding to protect ourselves when we are wounded is costly. Men who presume to be invulnerable in the exercise of power find it easy to treat with disdain what cannot wound. The first step in practicing vulnerability is simply to admit that one is susceptible to being wounded. Acknowledging vulnerability by sharing our pain with others is only possible if we have found a way to create community. When that bond is created, we may borrow power from communities that suffer with us. We are invited to live in the conviction that power and vulnerability are twin companions of every human soul as we deepen our faithfulness to God.

Do not fear, you worm Jacob, you
insect Israel!
 I will help you,
says the LORD; *your Redeemer is the*
Holy One
 of Israel.

Isaiah 41:14

EPILOGUE

When Jacob was very old and frail, he learned that his favorite son Joseph was still alive. His weary spirits were revived and Jacob determined to see Joseph before he died. On the way to meeting Joseph, God again appeared to Jacob to reassure him that the promises given long before in a different time would continue in his new home. "Then [God] said, 'I am God, the God of your father; do not be afraid to go down to Egypt, for I will make of you a great nation there. I myself will go down with you to Egypt, and I will also bring you up again; and Joseph's own hand shall close your eyes" (Gen. 46:3–4). With that promise in his heart, Jacob and all his offspring and livestock journeyed to Egypt, where he lived for seventeen years.

Jacob came face to face with Pharaoh, the ruler of Egypt, near the end of his life. "Pharaoh said to Jacob, 'How many are the years of your life?'" (We can only presume that Pharaoh asked that question because Jacob's appearance and the lines on his face revealed a life of pain and suffering.) "Jacob said to Pharaoh, 'The years of my earthly sojourn are one hundred thirty; few and hard have been the years of my life'" (Gen. 47:8–9). Despite his power and wealth, Jacob's life had been full of disappointment and loss, not at all what he dreamed in his youth. Whenever we measure the worth of a life by our dreams, there will be a residue of sadness and bitterness. Frederick Buechner imagines Jacob's feelings at the end of his life: "Even to this day I have tears in me to shed for Laughter's [Isaac] sorrow and for how I have always got the right hand and Esau always got the left yet how Esau always covered me with kisses even so."[1] Even when he won with trickery, Jacob lost.

Before Jacob died, he did three things: he extracted an oath from Joseph that he would bury him with his fathers in the cave in the field of Ephron the Hittite; he blessed Joseph's sons, Ephraim and Manasseh, giving his right hand to the younger son, Ephraim; and then he blessed (and cursed) his twelve sons. Jacob was frail but fiercely honest in judging and blessing (or not blessing) his twelve sons. "When Jacob ended his charge to his sons, he drew up his feet into the bed, breathed his last, and was gathered to his people" (Gen. 49:33). After his death, Jacob was embalmed. The Egyptians mourned his death for seventy days, and Joseph forgave his brothers who feared Joseph's revenge.

Perhaps the most remarkable illustration of Jacob's lifelong pattern of determination came near the end of his life. Miraculously, Jacob was reunited with Joseph, his favorite son, who had been sold into slavery by his brothers and whom Jacob had presumed to be killed by wild animals. "Israel [Jacob] said to Joseph, 'I did not expect to see your face; and here God has let me see your children also'" (Gen. 48:11). Joseph arranged his two sons before their grandfather to be blessed, the older at the right hand and the younger at the left hand. But Jacob crossed his arms and gave the greater blessing to the younger son, Ephraim. Even after Joseph had corrected his father, Jacob insisted on putting Ephraim ahead of Manasseh, his older brother. And so the persistence of Jacob established that for three generations, beginning with himself, the special blessing was not given to the eldest son who expected it. Jacob ended his life with clarity, judgment, some grace, and a little trickery. He died as ambiguously as he had lived.

The end of Jacob's life illustrates several dynamics of dying in faith that help us understand the importance of living toward death throughout our lives. First, we need assurance that the promises of God's faithfulness in life will remain in death. The quotation from Isaiah at the beginning of the epilogue referred to the people of Israel rather than the man Jacob. The promise is the same, however. When we feel small and helpless in the face of death, we need to remember that we are small in the faithful hands of God. That assurance of continuity in God makes it possible for us to face the discontinuity of death. We know that when we let go, God still holds on.

Second, when we near the end of life, we need to take care of "unfinished business" in our significant relationships. We do not know whether or how often Jacob had spoken honestly with his sons, many of whom had been a great disappointment. His judgments were honest and clear at the end, however. Blessing Ephraim was undoubtedly Jacob's most pleasurable act before dying. And he did it as he always had, with a little trickery. Even though there was the risk of displeasing his beloved son Joseph, Jacob did it anyway. Nearing death often creates freedom to act according to our deepest longings or desires.

Third, Jacob's life had not always been easy. At the end, however, there was a gracious surprise: he saw Joseph, the son beloved more than the others, whom he had thought was dead. As is sometimes the case with parents, Jacob's special love had endangered Joseph's life. We can only speculate that Jacob had berated himself through the years for his part in the loss of Joseph. Today, there are stories of fathers like Jacob whose special love for a child put that child at risk. The gracious gift at the end of life is an unexpected reunion. Often such a reconciliation is only possible as a surprise. Being reconciled at life's end is a gift that may cancel a lifetime of disappointments or heartache. In order to be open to surprise at the end of life, however, we need to learn to be vulnerable and practice dying while we are living.

PRACTICING DYING

We find life when we let it go. That is what it means to practice dying. In a culture that promotes possessing and holding on to as much as we can, that is not easy to do. The joke about men that "whoever has the most toys in the end wins" accurately illustrates the way this society measures a man's value by his possessions. The Christian story, however, is about dying to live. Jesus said it simply. Whoever wants to keep his life must lose it. The Christian life, therefore, is about letting go rather than holding on. It is about resting-in-neediness rather than self-sufficiency. "In the kingdom of Jesus," theologian Arthur McGill has written, "in the new kind of identity which he brings, where we are constantly receiving and never holding and possessing, where we are always looking to God for our reality, and not to ourselves, here human life is a *resting-in-neediness*, is a neediness that constitutes the character of our relationship to God."[2] We practice dying throughout life whenever we experience the pain of losing or letting go of people and things we love and cherish. It is the central characteristic of Christian faithfulness.

Theologian Ray S. Anderson has described how growing up on a farm next to a cemetery helped him understand the intimate connection between death and life. Although the cemetery was separated from his farm by a fence, he would play among the graves as a child. Frequently on a Sunday afternoon, his father would announce that he was going to tend the graves and invited others to go along. As he watered the flowers and cut the grass, he would rehearse the history of the community.

> I think we were lucky to live so near that cemetery. Our frequent walks through the grave sites and our conversations about the people buried there made them seem like old friends. The dead became a part of our lives; death seemed almost comfortable to us. At the same time, there was no preoccupation with death in our home. Because we lived with it each day, there seemed to be no need to live in fear of it.[3]

The life experience of growing up on a farm, raised by a father whose quiet belief in the goodness of God's creation included death, made it possible for Ray Anderson to understand that death is woven into the fabric of life. Grieving losses was as much a part of living as celebrating birthdays. We ought not be surprised by death even though its arrival is often unexpected. Modern men raised in towns and cities where death is removed from daily living will have a more difficult time practicing dying. When violent death occurs, we are likely to conclude that it is about violence instead of the ordinariness of death in life.

All of life is rehearsal for death. All the little losses we experience from birth are preparation for ultimate loss in death. When we describe ordinary loss in life as "a little death," we make the same point: learning to live and practicing dying are the same process. Morrie Schwartz, whose dying from ALS (sometimes called Lou Gehrig's disease) was made available to us through Mitch Albom's extraordinarily popular book *Tuesdays with Morrie*, wrote this in his own book *Letting Go: Morrie's Reflections on Living While Dying*. "Learn how to live, and you'll know how to die; learn how to die and you'll know how to live."[4] The difference between living and dying is not as great as we think. Sprinkled throughout the book are delightful aphorisms that support this fundamental connection between living and dying. Here is one: "Accept the past as past, without denying it or discarding it. Reminisce about it, but don't live in it. Learn from it, but don't punish yourself about it or continually regret it. Don't get stuck in it."[5] This wisdom about the unavoidable and vital connection between living and dying is part of the human story and the Christian story alike. However, it is not a part of the human story that men accept easily. For that reason, we need to identify ordinary practices that link dying in daily living.

DYING PRACTICES IN DAILY LIVING

If all of life is a rehearsal for death and if the best preparation for living fully is to be ready to die at any time, what are some of the ordinary ways by which men might "practice dying" as part of daily living? My intent is not to make life a morbid preoccupation with a fear of death but rather to diminish the terror of death by letting go of life as a daily practice. Each of these suggested practices invites men to consider dimensions of death and dying for the sake of living more fully. When we accept the reality that we are all living toward death, when we realize that everything we possess is fragile and contingent, we have new freedom for living. The moment we imagine keeping what we have forever, that feeling of freedom goes away and the anxieties of having come back. The following will help diminish the anxiety of living by practicing dying.

Get a yearly physical exam. Men resist having a physical examination on a regular basis. It is a modest form of denying death grounded on some notion of invulnerability. As a prostate cancer survivor, I am grateful for a persisting wife who would not allow me to ignore yearly trips to David Scheiner, M.D., who first detected the cancer. Men practice dying for the sake of living when they acknowledge their bodies are fragile enough to need regular checking.

Give someone a gift of one of your treasured possessions. When I retired from teaching at Catholic Theological Union, I was given gifts by several colleagues that were their own valued possessions. To receive such a gift is a wonderful honor, first of all, because it comes with a story about the meaning of the treasure. When we give away what we have, we prepare for dying by embodying a way of living that is shaped by letting go rather than holding on.

Tell your children about significant deaths in your family. When fathers are reluctant to tell their children about deaths in their lives, they make death a secret or something awful or shameful to be avoided. When fathers cannot talk about death with their children, they hand on to the next generation the same fearfulness about death that received from their fathers. When fathers tell their children about death and dying, they invite them to understand that death is a part of living.

Recycle regularly. The planet, like out bodies, is vulnerable and fragile. Recycling is dying practice because it reminds us that life is limited. Being committed to the continuity of the planet for the sake of our children's future is a way of living with the reality that there are limits. Finding ways to pass on books or other possessions when we no longer need them is another way to recognize human finitude. Death is the final limit. It is simply not true that "who has the most toys at the end wins."

Visit with someone who is dying. Being in the presence of someone who is dying is an encounter with helplessness and powerlessness that is often unsettling for men. There is nothing we can do to stop death. We can only share in the dying person's experience of powerlessness. When we walk with the dying, we are also reminded of our own mortality. While the aim in visiting a dying person is not to edify ourselves, avoiding being with those who are dying reinforces our discomfort with death in life.

Receive the Lord's Supper as often as possible. To share in the death and resurrection of Jesus in the Eucharist is a profoundly spiritual practice of dying. The One who invites us to receive his body and his blood in an ordinary meal of bread and wine is the same One, Jesus, who invites us to walk with him to the cross. The cross is the Christian symbol of faithfulness. It is the crossing of power and vulnerability for the sake of freedom, compassion, and abundant living. No other community practices dying as Christians do when they come together to study and pray. The golf club, the health club, the neighborhood pub, and a political caucus are all important places where men and women gather. The church, gathered about the cross in prayer, is the only place, however, that practices dying as a way of living. Men who long to discover their full humanity by practicing dying will be sustained for such faithful living by regular participation in the life of a church.

WONDER: THE BEGINNING OF FAITHFULNESS

Throughout this book, I have sought to fashion a vision of Christian faithfulness for men from a number of angles. The goal has been to invite men to reclaim their masculinity by developing more fully their humanity. The areas of men's undeveloped or underdeveloped abilities or capacities are the other side of practices men have been praised for in the past, even though they limited the full discovery of humanness. When men have difficulty expressing certain feelings, for example, it usually relates to the practice of self-control, for which men have been praised. Men have regarded emotions as dangerous because they may contaminate rational thinking or confuse the logic of choice. From that perspective, even admitting emotions that we control is risky. Although this view of reality no longer dominates the experience of men, men are still uncomfortable expressing intense emotion.

The recovery of wonder as part of Christian faithfulness invites men to live in the ambiguous tension between knowing and not knowing, between being on the way to fuller humanity and not yet being there. Wonder and amazement are the beginning of Christian faithfulness.

Epilogue

Being open to the wonder of God's surprise made it possible for me to be snatched out of retirement into a very rich and satisfying ministry I never imagined possible. We are astonished by the mysteries of living fully when we risk moving beyond traditional masculine stereotypes. Even in the middle of a life, men are sustained by communities of faith when they are invited to move out of the shadows of outdated masculinity, towards a deeper humanity, and into the fullness of faithful living.

NOTES

Introduction

1. Robert Bly, *Iron John: A Book about Men* (New York: Addison-Wesley, 1990).
2. Sam Keen, *Fire in the Belly: On Being a Man* (New York: Bantam Books, 1991), 102.
3. Edward Hirsch, "The Story of Jacob's Wrestling With an Angel," in *Genesis As It Is Written: Contemporary Writers on Our First Stories*, ed. David Rosenberg (New York: HarperSan Francisco, 1996), 188.

Prologue

1. David Steele, "The Jacob Cycle," *Theology Today* 37, no. 4 (January 1981): 461.
2. Kahlil Gibran, *The Prophet* (New York: Alfred A. Knopf, 1923), 17.
3. Frederick Buechner, *Son of Laughter: A Novel* (New York: HarperSan Francisco, 1993), 19–20.
4. Bly, *Iron John*, 6.
5. Susan Faludi, *Stiffed: The Betrayal of the American Man* (New York: William Morrow, 1999), 607.
6. Ellis Cose, *A Man's World: How Real Is Male Privilege—And How High Is Its Price?* (New York: HarperCollins, 1995), 2.

Chapter One: Handling Disappointment

1. Steele, "The Jacob Cycle," 466.
2. Langston Hughes, *The Dream Keeper and Other Poems* (New York: Alfred A. Knopf, 1994), 4.
3. Ted Bowman, *The Loss of Dreams: A Special Kind of Grief* (St. Paul, MN: personally published, 1994).
4. James Baldwin, review of *The Arrangement*, by Elia Kazan, *New York Review of Books*, March 23, 1967.
5. Steele, "The Jacob Cycle," 474.
6. Susan Faludi, "Rage of the American Male," *Newsweek*, August 16, 1999, 31.

Chapter Two: Acknowledging Vulnerability

1. Steele, "The Jacob Cycle," 479.
2. *Ibid.*, 478.
3. *Ibid.*, 478–479.
4. Dorothee Soelle, *Window of Vulnerability: A Political Spirituality*, trans. Linda M. Maloney (Minneapolis: Fortress Press, 1990), xi.
5. J. Christiaan Beker, *Suffering and Hope: The Biblical Vision and the Human Predicament* (Philadelphia: Fortress Press, 1987), 15.
6. Arthur C. McGill, *Death and Life: An American Theology*, ed. Charles A. Wilson and Per M. Anderson (Philadelphia: Fortress Press, 1987), 83.
7. Robert Coles, "An Interview with Robert Coles," *Second Opinion* (April, 1993): 58.
8. Avivah Gottlieb Zornberg, *The Beginning of Desire: Reflections on Genesis* (New York: Doubleday Image Books, 1995). Zornberg's description of "evening prayer" in Jacob's life connects easily with nighttime struggles of modern men. "Leaving all support systems behind him, Jacob moves into the world of the night. Here, nothing is clear, all is shifting, phantasm, illusion. And here, paradoxically, Jacob finds his ground of truth" (p. 188). When we sleep, we expect the unpredictable and we are vulnerable to interventions that are so deep they seem to come from God.

Chapter Three: Determination, Aggression, and Violence

1. Soelle, *Window of Vulnerability*, 9.
2. John Burnham Schwartz, *Reservation Road* (New York: Alfred A. Knopf, 1998), 195–196.
3. Herbert Anderson and Edward Foley, *Mighty Stories, Dangerous Rituals* (San Francisco: Jossey-Bass Publishers, 1998), 177.
4. *Ibid.*, 178.
5. Kitry Krause, "Men Who Beat Women," *Reader* 21, no. 14 (January 10, 1992): 29.
6. James Newton Poling, "Male Violence Against Women and Children," in *The Care of Men*, ed. Christie Cozad Neuger and James Newton Poling (Nashville: Abingdon Press, 1997), 139.
7. Don S. Browning, Bonnie J. Miller-McLemore, Pamela D. Couture, K. Brynolf Lyon, and Robert M. Franklin, *From Culture Wars to Common Ground: Religion and the American Family Debate*, 2nd ed. (Louisville: Westminster John Knox Press, 2000), 142.
8. Michael Janofsky, "New Columbine Killers' Tapes of Rage," *New York Times*, December 14, 1999.
9. Robert Moore and Douglas Gillette, *King, Warrior, Magician, Lover: Rediscovering the Archetypes of the Mature Masculine* (New York: HarperCollins, 1990), 75ff.

10. Robert J. Schreiter, *Reconciliation: Mission and Ministry in a Changing Social Order* (Maryknoll, NY: Orbis Books, 1992), 19.
11. Browning, et al., *Culture Wars*, 143.
12. *Peacemaking: The Believers' Calling* (New York: The General Assembly of the United Presbyterian Church in the United States of America, 1980).

Chapter Four: Expressing Feelings

1. Buechner, *Son of Laughter*, 15.
2. Deborah Tannen, "How to Close the Communication Gap Between Men and Women," *McCall's*, May 1991, 140.
3. Laura Doyle, *The Surrendered Wife* (New York: Simon and Schuster, 1999).
4. Simon Carr, "A Boy's World—Tears and All," in *Stories of Manhood: Journeys into the Hidden Hearts of Men*, ed. Steve Biddulph (Sydney: Finch Publishing, 2000), 9.
5. Philip L. Culbertson, *Counseling Men* (Minneapolis: Fortress Press, 1994), 13.
6. James D. Whitehead and Evelyn Eaton Whitehead, *Shadows of the Heart: A Spirituality of the Negative Emotions* (New York: Crossroad, 1995), 65.
7. *Ibid.*, 66.
8. Kent Haruf, *Plainsong* (New York: Vintage Books, 1999), 244.
9. *Ibid.*, 246.
10. Faludi, "Rage," 31.
11. Whitehead and Whitehead, *Shadows of the Heart*, 176.
12. *Ibid.*, 12.

Chapter Five: Promising

1. Barbara Dafoe Whitehead, *The Divorce Culture* (New York: Alfred A. Knopf, 1996), 4.
2. Herbert Anderson, Marie McCarthy, David Hogue, *Promising Again* (Louisville: Westminster John Knox Press, 1995), 25–31.
3. Pat Conroy, *Beach Music* (New York: Doubleday, 1995), 172.
4. Frank S. Pittman III, *Man Enough: Fathers, Sons, and the Search for Masculinity* (New York: G.P. Putnam's Sons, 1993), 128.
5. Michael Fishbane, *Text and Texture: Close Readings of Selected Biblical Texts* (New York: Schocken Books, 1979), 62.
6. Tex Sample, "Faith Commitment of the Heart," *Currents in Theology and Mission* 28, no. 2 (April 2001): 135.

Chapter Six: Paying Attention

1. Dave Barry, *Dave Barry's Complete Guide to Guys: A Fairly Short Book* (New York: Random House, 1995), 109.
2. Carol Gilligan, *In a Different Voice* (Cambridge: Harvard University Press, 1981), 8.
3. Joel Anderson, translator's introduction to *The Struggle for Recognition: The Moral Grammar of Social Conflicts*, by Axel Honneth (Cambridge, England: Polity Press, 1995), xi–xii.
4. Rainer Maria Rilke, *Rilke on Love and Other Difficulties*, ed. John Mood (New York: W.W. Norton, 1975), 28.
5. Joanna Trollope, *A Passionate Man* (New York: Berkley Books, 1990), 95.
6. Taylor Cox, Jr., *Cultural Diversity in Organizations: Theory, Research, and Practice* (San Francisco: Berrett-Koehler Publishers, 1993), 65.
7. Ernest Becker, *The Escape from Evil* (New York: The Free Press, 1975).
8. Kosuke Koyama, "Extend Hospitality to Strangers," *Currents in Theology and Mission* 20, no. 3, (1993): 173, 169.

Chapter Seven: Nurturing

1. David Blankenhorn, *Fatherless America: Confronting Our Most Urgent Social Problem* (New York: HarperCollins, 1995).
2. Joel Anderson, interview by Hugh LaFollette, *Ideas and Issues*, National Public Radio, January 25, 1998.
3. Moore and Gillette, *King, Warrior, Magician, Lover*, 98.
4. David Horsey, *Seattle Post-Intelligencer*, May 2, 2001.
5. The italicized sentences are the author's additions.
6. Selby Lighthill, "Generation," *Chicago Literary Review* (May 31, 1996): 9.
7. Blankenhorn, *Fatherless America*, 3.
8. Sandy and Harry Chapin, *Cat's in the Cradle* (Miami: Warner Bros. Publications U.S. Inc., 1974).
9. Herbert Anderson and Kenneth Mitchell, *Leaving Home* (Louisville: Westminster John Knox Press, 1993), 107–109.
10. Sidney Callahan, "How to Be Friends with Your Grown Children," *U.S. Catholic*, April 1993, 32.

Chapter Eight: Making and Keeping Friends

1. Martin E. Marty, *Friendship* (Allen, TX: Argus Communications, 1980), 7.
2. Robert D. Putnam, *Bowling Alone: The Collapse and Revival of American Community* (New York: Simon and Schuster, 2000).
3. Moore and Gillette, *King, Warrior, Magician, Lover*, 140.
4. Marty, *Friendship*, 11.
5. Dietrich Bonhoeffer, *Letters and Papers from Prison* (New York: Simon and Schuster, 1997), 388.
6. Frederick Buechner, *Godric* (New York: Atheneum, 1980), 48.

Chapter Nine: Learning to Grieve

1. Conroy, *Beach Music*, 603.
2. Samuel Osherson, *Wrestling with Love: How Men Struggle with Intimacy with Women, Children, Parents and Each Other* (New York: Fawcett Columbine, 1992), 299.
3. McGill, *Death and Life*, 61.
4. Culbertson, *Counseling Men*, 32.
5. Herbert Anderson, "Men and Grief: The Hidden Sea of Tears without Outlet," in *The Care of Men*, ed. Christie Cozad Neuger and James Newton Poling (Nashville: Abingdon Press, 1997). Material in this chapter is drawn from this previous essay.
6. C. S. Lewis, *A Grief Observed* (New York: Seabury Press, 1961), 12.
7. *Ibid.*, 13, 22, 23.
8. Cose, *A Man's World*, 9.
9. *Ibid.*, 10.

Chapter Ten: Sharing Power

1. Arthur Brittan, *Masculinity and Power* (Oxford, England: Basil Blackwell, 1989), 5.
2. Dennis H. Wrong, *Power: Its Forms, Bases and Uses* (New York: Harper and Row, 1980), 2.
3. James Newton Poling, *The Abuse of Power: A Theological Problem* (Nashville: Abingdon Press, 1991), 23.
4. Pauline Kleingeld, "Just Love? Marriage and the Question of Justice," *Social Theory and Practice* 24, no. 2 (summer 1998): 269.
5. Rita Nakashima Brock, *Journeys by Heart: A Christology of Erotic Power* (New York: Crossroad, 1988), xv.

Epilogue

1. Buechner, *Son of Laughter*, 273.
2. McGill, *Death and Life*, 83.
3. Ray S. Anderson, *Unspoken Wisdom: Truths My Father Taught Me* (Minneapolis: Augsburg Fortress, 1995), 112.
4. Morrie Schwartz, *Letting Go: Morrie's Reflections on Living While Dying* (New York: Walker and Company, 1996), 125.
5. *Ibid.*, 53.

ABOUT THE AUTHOR

Herbert Anderson was born in Belvedere, Illinois, in 1936, and ordained in the Lutheran Church in America (now the Evangelical Lutheran Church in America) in 1962. He received a B.A. degree from Gustavus Adolphus College in St. Peter, Minnesota, a B.D. from Augustana Seminary (now the Lutheran School of Theology in Chicago), and a Ph.D. from Drew University, Madison, New Jersey. Anderson has penned numerous articles and books on subjects ranging from a theology for the seriously ill to handling loss and grief, living alone, and theology and pastoral care of families. He has served as both pastor and professor throughout his career, including a teaching period at Princeton Theological Seminary from 1969 to 1975. Presently he is Director of Pastoral Care and Congregational Life at St. Mark's Episcopal Cathedral in Seattle and Visiting Professor of Pastoral Theology at Seattle University, where his wife, Phyllis (a Lutheran pastor), is Associate Dean and Director of the Institute for Ecumenical Theological Studies. The Andersons have two children and three grandchildren.